MW00976726

Just Joey

A Novel

CINDY VICTOR

To Michelle Barrett, MD~
With much gratitude
for the thoughtful care you
give your patients~
Cindy Victor

Copyright © 2014 Cindy Victor

All rights reserved.

ISBN: 1499328028

ISBN 13: 9781499328028

Library of Congress Control Number: 2014908487

CreateSpace Independent Publishing Platform

North Charleston, South Carolina

Dedication

To my son, Frank, who shares the love of all my dogs.

Acknowledgments

For their help and support with this book, I am grateful to Howard Steinberg, Barbara Keller, Jo Langer, Sheila Zitur-Kuehn, and my husband, Gary. I am also grateful for the three wonderful German shepherd dogs who shared our home and gave us years of happiness.

Contents

First Love

It was a Friday afternoon last October when I had to put down an Amazon parrot called Federico that could recite Garcia-Lorca poetry in both Spanish and English. Then a German shepherd dog that had got its tail slammed in a car door was brought into the clinic. A broken tail is forever, so I felt sick about the shepherd. It didn't help that the dog was a black and tan with a stoic bearing and sorrowful eyes that glowed honey-brown—a heart-wrenching resemblance to Joey.

I thought the afternoon couldn't get worse, but it did. At four o'clock I had to put down the ancient Yugoslavian mountain hound that had been my patient since I hung out my shingle in Minot seven years ago.

This was not a typical day at Magic Minot Veterinary Clinic. If it had been, I'd be doing something else for a living.

Finally, I got to go home to Dee and the kids, and mercifully I arrived to find them out grocery shopping. Except for our four dogs, I had the house to myself. This is such a rare occurrence that its happening usually makes me feel adventuresome and very much a boy. But this afternoon I felt like a tired old man—until, that is, the dogs, having been out in back, came one by one through the kitchen doggy door to greet me. I sank gratefully to one thirty-five-year-old knee, to be licked by Ginger, pawed by Corky, and nuzzled by Sandy. Staring at me with a tongue-lolling grin, Nipper let his penis show, slick and red. For Nipper that's a sure sign of happiness, and I was cheered.

After greeting me and each other—as if they hadn't been together all day—the dogs plopped to the floor or wandered off. I sat down at the table and rested my eyes on Ginger, who is mostly-boxer, a breed that a poet or breeder once described as "most beautiful ugliness." The description fits Ginger to a T, and also fits this small North Dakota city, a city that Joey briefly knew. It's called Magic Minot in Chamber of Commerce literature.

And so I had all this: family, great home in a great town, four pooches, rewarding career, health, memories, a bottle of beer in the fridge. A crappy day? Maybe not. But how many Federicos, or Yugoslavian mountain hounds for that matter, am I likely to know in my life? And that tail, that tail!

The day's mail was on the table. Nothing but junk, I thought, until I found the pink envelope that I recognized as coming from Keystone, South Dakota. A letter from Chappie. She and Stephen must have a new puppy. It had to be that because it wasn't time for a birthday, anniversary, or Christmas letter from Chappie. She and I were still close, but because she disliked emailing and disdained texting, our communications were ritualized.

I tore open the envelope. Hah! I'd guessed right. They'd gotten Rumpkin (what a weird nickname for a kid) a puppy for his sixth birthday. Chappie's words were, "Come and check this one out. We're all gaga over him."

Of course I'd go. It's a sacrosanct tradition that when either of us acquires a new puppy, the other one gets on a plane. You fly alone, or with your spouse, or with your spouse plus kids. But you go see the pup. I read on:

"Rumpkin couldn't decide on a name for him, so Stephen and I decided to call him Joey."

I felt shocked. Their giving Joey's name to another dog seemed a travesty. But excitement was still my chief response to the letter, and as always when I hear from Chappie, I wished I could call her.

I imagined myself with her right this minute, telling her, "Chappie, my day was just hell. I had to euthanize two wonderful patients and what happened to another you don't want to know."

She'd write a consoling response on a piece of paper from the notepad that hangs on a ribbon or chain around her neck. Chappie writes small. Stephen jokes that *he* should wear a magnifying glass on a chain.

I really learned to read from Chappie's notes. She printed them for me, as I imagine she does now for Rumpkin. When I was very young and she printed, she made her letters straight up and down—the ones with closed loops looking like balloons on sticks. At first, I would stare at her while she printed, noticing her hair (the color of butterscotch custard), the curve of her lashes, the perfection of her tanned legs. She lived in shorts, T-shirts, thick white socks, and canvas sneakers. I would feel a queer ache behind my ears if the little notepad dangled over one of her small breasts. It sometimes did that.

I reread the letter. Chappie didn't say, but the puppy must be a black and tan shepherd, otherwise she wouldn't have named him Joey. I was trying not to mind the name. It isn't important, I told myself. Besides, it was just so great that I was going to see Chappie.

Rising to get the lone bottle of beer, I felt antsy to talk to my travel agent. It was after six. What was she doing, buying out the whole grocery store?

I came back to the table, where Chappie's three-page pink letter lay at the center of the clutter of mail. I saluted it with my bottle of Pilsner Urquell. Now it was a day. Now it was some kind of day.

Just five minutes into my afternoon flight, I let my paperback novel fall closed and fell into my own story—mine, Chappie's, and Joey's.

It all began in Long Beach, California, at a community hospital situated on a low hill that caught the smell of the Pacific Ocean on the November morning of my birth. My mother imparted this information to me while driving me to the same hospital the night of my sixth birthday.

We lived in an old stucco house in Belmont Shore, where many of the homeowners had come from Iowa. It was a small house, but of course it seemed large to me. Moreover, it had such interesting things as a stained-glass window in the living room, a diner-style booth with red vinyl seats in the breakfast room, and a wrought-iron gate where the front porch started, for me to swing on.

Our block was so close to the beach that ocean smells played a bigger part in my life than aromas of my mother's cooking, or scents from her flower beds.

My mother was beautiful, and my father was big and strong. I loved them, and the beach, and I desperately feared dogs.

My friend Bill, who lived next door, had a dog. The fearsome springer spaniel was named Edith Grace, after Bill's unmarried aunts in Iowa whom Bill's dad called "real dogs." When I played at Bill's house, Edith Grace was kept outside, tied to a tree in the front yard or loose in the backyard. If Bill and I decided to go out back to play, Bill's mother took Edith Grace in, being extremely careful not to let the dog near me.

The climax of my relationship of avoidance with the spaniel came one November evening when I'd been coloring pictures with Bill in his kitchen. Bill's dad had come home from work at his car lot and, not knowing I was there, had let the dog in. Singing and dancing his way into the kitchen that evening, this father so unlike mine was holding a straw hat aloft in one hand and a cane in the other.

This interesting return home of Bill's father inspired such a heady mix of awe and confusion in me that I didn't notice Edith Grace until she jumped up and licked my arm. Screaming, I climbed onto the kitchen table. Even after Bill's mother rushed the dog back outside, I kept on bellowing.

The climax was Bill's dad shouting, "Shut up! Shut the hell up! Get off that table and go home, you moron! You're crazy, and stupid, and I don't want you here anymore!"

As I ran to the front door I heard Bill's dad tell Bill's mom, "Tina and Lawrence need parenting classes. Better yet, they should get the kid a lobotomy."

At home, my father condemned Bill's father as a jerk and a drunk, then went next door. When he returned he announced that I wasn't to play at Bill's ever again.

The next day, my mother took me shopping and we bought three picture books about dogs. On subsequent days she bought me coloring and connect-the-dot books featuring dogs. I understood the motive behind these gifts, but I didn't feel insulted or threatened by them. In fact, I liked them all.

But dog-themed gifts wouldn't do the intended job.

Didn't my parents know that dogs made of paper weren't the same as those with slick long teeth and hot dripping tongues and clammy noses that could smell a boy's fear even from across the street? Why weren't other people afraid of dog eyes? In picture books dog eyes were soft, warm, looking away at a butterfly or down at a food bowl. But in real life dog eyes were dark pools of cunning thought. *I'll pretend I can't jump over this fence I'm behind, and when you walk by I'll jump over it and tear you to pieces. I'll lie still with my eyes closed so you'll think I'm asleep, and when you let down your guard I'll attack and tear you to pieces.*

A stuffed collie that I thought beautiful, and that I named Lassie, was the last thing my mother bought me before my sixth birthday, which came on Saturday, one week to the day after the big scene at Bill's house.

I woke with an earache the morning of my birthday. Feeling grumpy as well as ill, I went to the kitchen and accepted my mother's and father's hugs. "Well, what do you think you're getting for your birthday, champ?" my father asked.

I felt half wounded, half anticipatory. Surely my parents realized how hard it was for me not to have Bill to play with anymore. Weren't they going to do something about it? Not even on my birthday? "I don't know," I answered. "I guess a toy, or a shirt."

"A *shirt?*" My mother squealed this as if no boy ever got a shirt for his birthday.

"Well, it could be a shirt," my father said. "Or socks. How about mittens and ear muffs for when we go visit your South Dakota relatives?"

I didn't answer, although going to South Dakota, where I would build a snowman and ride downhill on a sled, was something I wanted to do. I decided not to tell about the pain in my ear. If I did, my mother would take my temperature, and if I had a fever, there'd be no chance of playing with Bill today.

Beaming at me, my parents made me cover my eyes. "You're not peeking, are you?" my mother asked. I shook my head no—the movement adding to the dull pain that plagued my ear. Squinting into the red-black darkness behind my lids and hands, I hoped that I had to do this so Bill could be sneaked into the kitchen.

"Happy birthday, Gary," my mother said. "You can open your eyes now."

I blinked my eyes open. They froze in a wide stare. I turned halfway toward my mother and almost reached for her hand.

"It's your birthday puppy," she said happily. "Look at him. Isn't he the most adorable puppy you ever saw?"

"His name's Joey," said my father, holding the squirming dog just a few feet away from me. It didn't look like a puppy and obviously it wanted to get to me. The very second that my dad let go, that dog was going to lunge.

My mother said, "You and Daddy will build a doghouse together, and when Daddy comes home from work at night we'll all walk him together."

"If you don't like the name Joey, we can change it," my father said. "That's what they called him at the shelter, though, so he's used to it."

I didn't move or speak. The dog—mostly black with enormous ears and paws—wriggled and whined impatiently, aching to jump on me and bite me.

"He's twelve weeks old already," my mother said. "That's why he's so big. But isn't he cute? He's a German shepherd. He's still a puppy, honey. Puppyhood lasts till a dog's one year old."

I'd caught a sharp breath that smelled of dog when she said German shepherd. Those were vicious! They were attack dogs!

"German shepherds are so smart and gentle that they're trained to guide blind people," my father said.

I still hadn't said a word. I didn't dare.

"Should I take him out in the yard?" my father asked. "Would you rather play with him there?"

He'd gone from bending over the dog to holding it in place while squatting behind it. Not once had the so-called puppy stopped trying to wriggle away so it could get to me. Nor had it taken its eyes from my eyes for that matter. And it was big. It seemed to be growing even as I stared at it. A few more minutes and it would be too big for my dad to hold onto.

"Sweetheart? You're not afraid of him, are you? Not this darling little puppy? He's so gentle." My mother said this while gently rubbing my back.

"You can't be afraid of *this* dog," my father chimed in. "This is your birthday puppy."

I felt angry. Was I acting afraid? Did I run away or make noises like I was scared? No! Not at all. And to prove I wasn't a coward, I said, "Let him go."

"My father grinned. "Okay, champ. Brace yourself. Puppies move fast."

My mother withdrew her hand from my back.

I stood facing the dog. It struggled against the hands holding it in place. What was my father waiting for? Was he scared, too? Both my parents were close enough to save me if the dog attacked, but they'd have to pry its jaws from my throat.

My dad let go. The dog lunged as I'd known it would. It licked me all over my face. Also on my throat, hands, ankles, feet—every part of me not covered by pajamas. When I fell over backward, it really got its licks in.

"Are you okay?" my mother asked.

I couldn't answer. If I opened my mouth I'd have dog tongue in it. I heard my father softly say, "He's fine."

After managing to turn over, I crawled like a baby—a very fast-moving baby—out of the kitchen to the breakfast room. That the dog didn't grab my foot to stop me told me that my father was restraining it again. I sat on the edge of the booth bench, my bare feet hanging down. I didn't pull my legs up, and was proud of that.

My mother came to stand in the arched entrance to the breakfast room. "Joey's just so eager to be your friend. When he licks you he's kissing you. He'll calm down, honey, when he's used to us. Puppies sleep most of the time."

"Let him go again!" I called to my father, my wealth of new-found courage making me sit taller. My mom's smile widened as she moved out of the way.

I expected it to be like a train coming through the house straight at me. But Joey trotted into the breakfast room, came to a standstill in front of me, and laid his head on my knees. My mother said, "Oh, honey, he *loves* you."

I stroked him thoughtfully, using just the tips of my fingers. "I like his ears," I said.

"Do you like the name Joey? Is it all right? He sort of looks like a Joey, don't you think?"

"Unhuh." I didn't want to talk, and I didn't want her to talk. I was thinking that I wasn't a coward anymore, and that more than anything in the world I wished Bill could see me petting my very own attack dog.

"Gary," my father said from the doorway. "Bill's here."

I looked up startled. Bill, who was heavy like his mother and never smiled very much, appeared in the doorway with a gift-wrapped box in his arms. He widened his mouth crookedly.

"Hi," I said. "Do you like him? His name's Joey. He's a German shepherd."

Joey shifted his gaze and slowly moved his tail back and forth, but he didn't lift his head from my knees.

"He's neat," Bill said.

I went on stroking my dog. "He'll be a giant when he's grown," I told Bill.

"Well, I'll never know. We have to move back to Iowa. My dad hates it here. He says it's scummy. He says it's full of people who don't belong here. He says they ruined it."

I shrugged. It didn't faze me that Bill was going away. Joey was here now and would always be here. Anyhow, Bill was a witness to my victory over fear, and he knew what I owned; he wasn't needed any more.

My fingers moved from Joey's forehead to one of his sleeked-back ears, softer than anything I'd ever felt before. Touching this dog made me feel that nothing at all could hurt me. Not ever. As a matter of fact, my earache was gone. I put a hand to my ear and pressed. Gone. Completely gone.

"Honey, do you have an earache," my mother asked.

I shook my head no, not looking at her. I wished Joey and I were alone together. In a sense, we were, but the others didn't know that and their not knowing made it less important.

"I'm going to make breakfast," my mother said. "Bill, let me put your present for Gary on the table. It's wrapped so nice! I can't imagine what it is. Would you like to have some cereal with us, honey? Or toast and jam?"

"No thanks. Gary, guess what? Edith Grace threw up this morning in front of the washing machine. My dad didn't see it and he stepped in it, barefoot. It squished all between his toes."

I couldn't take my eyes off Joey's head on my knees to respond to this news, but I knew that I should show polite interest, so I murmured, "Really?"

The thing I couldn't get over was that all this stuff was going on—Bill's coming over, everybody's talking, my mom's coming in and out of the room—and Joey hadn't once lifted his head from my lap.

With the flat of my palm, I stroked the side of Joey's mouth.

You love me, don't you Joey?

For an answer, Joey licked my fingers. And so he became my dog.

CHAPTER 2

Our Eyes Played Tricks On Us

That morning after Bill went home, my mother asked if I wanted Joey, who was already housebroken, to sleep in my bedroom. "But not in your bed, honey. We'll put a blanket on the floor for him, right next to your bed."

That night I added Joey's name to my routine God blesses, after "And God bless my cousin Alan in South Dakota."

Alan had been ill for as long as I could remember. Praying for him sometimes made me imagine God, who lived, as I figured it, way up in the sky over California, zooming straight to South Dakota to make him well. I had asked my mom if God might really do this some night, and she'd answered with tears in her eyes that she didn't see why he wouldn't.

But one night I'd been in a fooling around mood at bedtime, and had asked God to bless my cousin Alan and make his lukie lukie go away.

My mother's swift response had mortified me. "Sweetie, don't say that again, ever. Say leukemia. It's too important to give it a funny name." Then she leaned down to kiss my cheek, but I lay stiff as a board, not wanting her kiss. How could I have known the importance of leukemia if no one had told me? Had she ever said that Alan was sicker than kids who had colds, or flu, or chicken pox as the Steinberg twins down the block had had, or earaches?

But I'd known, deep down, how serious leukemia was, because my mother often looked weepy after talking to Aunt Ellen or Uncle Ray on the phone. Even so, I stayed angry with her that night, until she left my room. I'd been noticing for some time that shame came accompanied by anger.

The night I turned six I ended my prayers with, "And God bless Joey, who's my best friend forever and ever," to see how she'd take that. Maybe she thought that she, and not Bill, had been my best friend before Joey came.

She said, "That's nice. And you're Joey's best friend, too."

After she left the room, I forced myself to stay awake long after my eyes turned grainy. Finally, murmurings and other soft sounds from the living room warned me to act as if asleep.

On their way down the hall, my parents paused by my open door. I breathed deeply and rhythmically. When they continued on their way, I continued being quiet. Their bedroom door was also kept open at night in case I called.

Slipping out of bed, I wakened Joey by petting him above his nose and around his chin. He raised his head. His eyes on mine in the hazy dark glowed like honey in a jar.

He yawned, and guessing what I wanted, he rose to his feet and with my help climbed onto the bed. I thought it was a good thing he could do most of the work himself, because there was no way I could lift that great big puppy.

In bed together, on our sides, sharing a pillow, we lay facing the opened doorway beyond which a night light illuminated the hall. I had an arm around Joey's middle and fell asleep on a stream of happy plans. I would run on the beach with Joey. I'd teach him to fetch. He would go with my parents and me to visit the South Dakota relatives, who lived in Keystone, in the Black Hills. With my cousins Karen and Alan, we would play in the snow. My mom and dad, and Aunt Ellen and Uncle

Ray—all beaming happiness—would watch us run and jump in the snow. Alan would fling snow over his head and shout, "My lukie lukie's gone! My lukie lukie's gone!"

I woke in a bed that was rattling crazily, and thinking we were having an earthquake, I sprang to my knees. But it was Joey making the bed shake. His head banging on the headboard was the cause of the noise.

I leaned over to see him better. His mouth and one exposed eye were stretched so wide that it must have hurt terribly, and his head repeatedly striking the headboard seemed certain to knock him unconscious or even kill him.

I grabbed his thrashing head and tried to move it, but accomplished nothing more than getting my fingers slick with his saliva. I wiped them on my pajamas, then repositioned my hands on Joey's head and tried again.

Pain pierced my left hand. I yanked both hands from him and tucked them under my chin. Blood trickled down to my wrist. Joey kept shaking—his mouth wide open and his head bumping against the headboard. "Joey, stop it stop it stop it," I begged. I clapped my hands to my face and the pain in my palm intensified. I was in such great fear for Joey that I didn't cry. Wouldn't he ever stop? I threw myself over him, pressing down on his body with mine.

It worked. He stopped doing everything. For a long moment all I felt was the rise and fall of our chests—mine on top of Joey's. Then I felt him lick my hand. He licked it all around the part that hurt so much.

"Gary!" my mother cried, as light filled the bedroom.

"He's all right," said my father as he snatched me up in his arms.

"No, Lawrence, he's been bitten!"

In my father's arms, I looked down at Joey, who sort of jumped, slid, and fell off the bed. With his big ears flattened and out to the sides, he dashed from the room. I wanted to call him back, but was stopped by my mother's cries. "There's blood all over him. I'm calling an ambulance!"

In a calm voice, my dad said, "The blood's from his hand. There are no wounds on his face."

"Oh, thank God for that. I'll run water over his hand. We'll have to take him to the emergency room."

Her mention of running water caused a sudden urge in my penis, plus a new concern about Joey's comfort. "I have to go let Joey out," I said, thinking we would pee together. But instead of putting me down, my father carried me across the hall to the bathroom. There, he set me on my feet. I looked up at him and said, "Joey has to go outside."

As if I hadn't spoken, my dad said, "Let me see that hand, Gary."

I felt slighted. Even a housebroken puppy needs the bathroom when it wakes from sleeping. I knew this intuitively. I knew also, from experience, that a child can be at one and the same time the center of attention and totally ignored.

My mother ran warm water over my hand and wrist. "There's only one puncture," she said. "Do you see? Joey bit him but didn't close his mouth. It could have been a hundred times worse. It looks like it's almost stopped bleeding."

"Joey didn't bite me!" I yelled when she stopped talking. "His head was shaking and my hand got in the way!"

"Calm down, Gary. It's all right now." My father gently rubbed a washcloth over my face while my mom patted my hand dry around the wound, then wrapped my hand round and round with gauze.

"I have to go, and Joey has to go, too," I whined. "I keep telling you and you don't listen to me."

My mother murmured soothingly, "All right, honey. Let me pull your jammies down for you. Daddy will let Joey outside. Then we're taking you to the hospital."

The hospital! They were making this too serious.

"All finished?" She flushed the toilet, making me feel like a baby. "Let's get you into something warm and—"

My dad broke in with, "Gary, can you tell us what exactly happened?"

Finally. I took a deep breath, then said, "Joey was shaking the bed. He was shaking all over. His mouth was wide open like he was screaming. Only he wasn't. He bit me, but he didn't mean to. That's what happened. Now let Joey out, *please.*"

Without a word my father left the bathroom.

My mother gave me little kisses all over my face, and on the top of my head, while telling me repeatedly that everything would be all right and I shouldn't be upset.

My dad came back wearing a jacket and carrying jackets for us. He also had my mom's purse. "You were right, Gary. Joey really needed to go."

"Did you let him back in?" I asked, feeling righteous.

"I sure did. Tina, if you can manage alone with Gary—"

"You'll take Joey?" she asked.

"Yes."

I heard sadness in that, and hoped it wasn't a bad sign. Perhaps it meant he wasn't angry at Joey, that he pitied him and wanted him to be well.

"You know how to get to Community, Tina?"

She answered that she did. Only then did I realize I was going one place and Joey to another. "Where's Joey going?" I demanded.

"To an animal hospital that's open all night," answered my father.

"Are you going to leave him there?"

"I don't know. The doctor will decide that."

But that wasn't fair. The doctor didn't know how frightened and unhappy Joey would be if he wasn't in his own home with the boy who owned him. I wanted to explain this to them, but feeling myself start to cry, I ducked my head down and didn't talk.

In the car with my mother, I could smell the ocean. I imagined a dog, one that looked like Joey, wandering lost and sad on the wet sand at water's edge. That poor dog wished its owner would come running up to it and say, "Here you are. I've looked all over for you. Let's get you home, boy."

In the hospital, I sat on a table under a bright light. A nurse removed the gauze from my hand. "What kind of dog is it?" she asked, bending over her work.

"A German shepherd," my mother answered. "We got him at the pound, but we think he's a purebred."

The nurse looked up. "There's blood, but I don't see a puncture. I don't see anything. Let's clean it off so I can get a better look."

She said this might sting a little. I braced myself for pain, but there wasn't any.

"There's nothing there!" cried my mother. "I saw the puncture and so did my husband."

"I didn't," I announced.

This was true, but I knew I'd been bitten. Hush, said a voice within. Don't tell what you know.

A man dressed in green from head to foot came and joined the conversation between my mom and the nurse. He said that Joey might have been scratching himself and had scratched so hard that he drew blood. "Puppies have sharp enough toenails to gouge furniture and doors, let alone cut their own skin," he said knowingly.

My knowledge threatened to burst out of me in an explosion of words. *You're wrong! You don't know anything about it. Joey's tooth went right inside my hand. And his legs were all sticking straight out. He wasn't scratching himself. And he did bite me. I know he did because it hurt really bad. And there was lots of blood!*

But I held it all in.

"So you really thought you'd been bitten by a dog, huh?" asked the nurse, giving me a sly smile.

"His birthday dog," said my mother, smiling too. "Joey is Gary's birthday dog."

My father came out to the driveway when we drove up. "Joey's here, too," was his greeting to me. "He's in your room, fast asleep."

In the dark of my bedroom, I looked down at my big, sleeping puppy and thought of the German shepherd that, before its owner had found it and taken it home, had wandered lost and scared on the beach. I didn't kneel to touch Joey, because he'd had a lot of excitement and needed his rest.

My mom and dad and I sat in the breakfast room drinking milk and eating birthday cake even though it was the middle of the night. We all spoke softly, perhaps not to wake Joey, or perhaps because we were up after midnight.

My dad told us what had happened at the animal hospital. A technician checked Joey out and said that as far as he could tell, the dog had nothing at all wrong with him. He didn't think Joey had had a seizure, because dogs that young never do.

"He told me all about canine epilepsy. It's not uncommon, but it doesn't ever start this early."

"Then Joey really was just scratching himself," my mother said.

"I guess, but they couldn't find any cuts on him. That's the darndest thing, because we do know there was blood."

"From Joey biting my hand," I reminded them. Then I remembered that I wasn't going to talk about it.

"No, you weren't bitten," my father said with conviction. "We just thought we saw a puncture wound. Our eyes played tricks on us."

"I see a sleepy six-year-old," said my mother. "And my eyes aren't playing tricks on me." She was right. I could hardly wait to be in bed, near Joey, who'd bitten me, but of course without meaning to.

CHAPTER 3

Leaving God And The Angels

I could see why the old people who moved into Bill's empty house on Valentine's Day were called Mr. And Mrs. Mooney. The wife, who wore pale shimmery sweaters that reflected the sun, had the sliver shape of a quarter moon. Whenever I looked at her in profile, I imagined the invisible rest of her, the round-ness that I couldn't see but would bump into if I tried to pass through it.

Mr. Mooney, also bespectacled, had a round face that was encircled by white hair except on the very top. He was the moon when it's almost but disappointingly not quite whole.

My mother related at dinner the day the Mooneys moved in that Mr. Mooney was a retired minister and Mrs. Mooney had been the church organist. I didn't want to go with my mother that afternoon when she took the Mooneys a potted geranium and a plate of heart-shaped lemon cookies. I hadn't been inside Bill's house since the day of the big blow up, and didn't intend to go back. So that afternoon I'd played down the block at the Steinberg twins', and while my mother learned all about the Mooneys, I learned all about death.

"Mrs. Mooney is simply wonderful," said my mother. "She fell a year-and-a-half ago and broke her hip, but today you wouldn't know it if you didn't see her get up and walk. She moves slowly and uses a cane out of doors, but so do lots of older people who haven't been through half of what she's been through. Both their sons dying, one nineteen and one twenty. One was in the infantry, and one on a patrol boat in the Mekong Delta. He was lost in the Mekong River. Can you imagine, Lawrence?"

What was this? A son of the people who lived in Bill's house had drowned in a river? Oh, I would tell this to Howard Steinberg, who just today had said that drowned people swell up like balloons and float on the water until someone finds them. His twin, Barbara, who had a cold and was sucking two cherry cough drops at one time, had added, "Peoble who drowd id the ocea cad fload all the way to Chida."

My mother turned her attention to Joey, lying under the table. "Joey, out," she said. "Out now, sweetie. You're too grown up to be under there when we're eating."

She had this one-way conversation with Joey almost every night, and Joey always cooperated by removing himself to the kitchen. One evening in April, as we were having dinner in the breakfast room, Joey got out from under the table at the same time the phone rang in the kitchen. My mother went to answer it. "Oh, Ellen," I heard her cry before she burst into tears.

My dad got up and went to the kitchen. I remained where I was. I knew that my cousin Alan had died. And I knew, having had many discussions on the subject with the Steinberg twins, who were eight, exactly what death was. You couldn't do anything more on Earth after dying, not even think, so you were put in a wood box that was fancy on the inside, and the box, called a casket, was put in the ground. Worms got into the casket and ate you, but so what? Nothing could hurt you anymore. Snakes eating you wouldn't hurt.

But there was a part of you that nothing could eat. It was your immortal soul, and it was invisible, like the part of Mrs.

Mooney that couldn't be seen. It went to heaven, zooming straight up through layers of thin sky and thick cloud until it got there. Then, in heaven, it became the whole you! That immortal soul looked just the way you did when you were on Earth! And God and everybody else in heaven could see you, and you could see them, because no one was invisible in heaven.

Alan must have started his journey to heaven while I'd been eating chicken noodle soup. I pictured that trip: Alan invisible, wearing an invisible long white robe, his feet bare. He'd kicked, as if swimming, to make himself go faster.

And now Alan was visible again and able to do everything: breathe, eat, talk, walk, throw a ball. Everything except come back.

Did you want to leave God and the angels and come back to your family? The twins hadn't said. Anyway, how would they know? How would anybody, except dead people.

I had known my cousin only from photographs and talking on the phone. Every picture of Alan sent by his parents had elicited the same response from my mother: "You boys look *so* much alike. Anyone would think you were brothers, not cousins."

I had thought so too, and probably Alan had noticed how alike we were when he saw pictures of me. It was a shame that we hadn't met face to face to see if we would feel like brothers. But at least Alan could think about me up in heaven. And when I went to South Dakota and played with Alan's sister in the snow, he could look down and watch.

The day before we were to go to South Dakota for Alan's funeral, I woke with a sore throat, achy muscles, and a fever. When it was decided that my father would go alone, I felt bitter disappointment. Finally I'd had a chance to fly in a plane, and to see snow, but a cold had snatched it away from me. Aunt Ellen, on the phone, had told my mom that Keystone was having its usual spring snowstorm.

"If I take medicine right now the cold might disappear," I reasoned when I heard this weather report. My mother answered that only time can cure a cold—about two weeks of time, from start to finish.

I felt some relief despite how much I had wanted to go. If we all went to Keystone, Joey would have to be left at the veterinary clinic, which was also a kennel. I couldn't see how it was different for a dog to be in a kennel than in the pound.

My father had never left us alone before. More than once I'd heard my mother say how grateful she was that his profession (she always called it his profession, not his job) didn't require travel, or long hours at an office.

With its biggest and only deep-voiced human gone from it, our house seemed strange, and larger. I felt a sense of loss. For the first time, I considered what it must be like for Aunt Ellen and Uncle Ray and Cousin Karen not to have Alan with them anymore.

"It's kind of fun, our being alone together, isn't it?" asked my mother while tucking me into bed the first night. "I haven't spent one night without your daddy since we were married. Not one. I thought I'd hate it, but it's sort of an adventure."

I felt shocked. Where was her loyalty? Didn't she know that my father might become lost in a snowstorm and freeze to death? Or that he might die in a plane crash on his way home? "I miss him," I announced firmly, afterwards searching her eyes for signs of contrition.

She smiled. "I do too."

Oh, no, she didn't. Not after what she'd just said.

"I love Daddy more than I love you," I said. Instantly the light faded from her eyes, but just as quickly it returned. Even so, the smile she gave me was not the same.

After an unbearable silence, she said, "That's all right. I understand your feeling that way, honey. Your daddy is the finest man in the whole world. He deserves the best of your love. So don't worry about it, not even for a minute."

Her words made me feel worse. I hated myself.

When she left the room, and I heard her go in the living room, I climbed out of bed and stretched out on the floor next to Joey. Since the night of my sixth birthday, I'd wondered if my having taken Joey into my bed against my mom's wishes had caused him to have that fit. I was never going to risk finding out. Besides, Joey was trained to stay off furniture. My dad said that when people allowed dogs to do things they were trained not to do, the dogs got all confused and then were unhappy.

Lying half on Joey's blanket and half on the carpet, I pressed my face against Joey's neck, which had thickened considerably since we got him and was, I believed, strong as steel. My arm around Joey's middle rose and fell with his steady breathing. I wished I hadn't been mean to my mom. What she'd said was sort of true, about it being an adventure for us, but I couldn't go to the living room and admit that to her.

Snuggling closer to Joey, I said a silent prayer that nothing bad would happen to either of my parents, because I loved and needed both of them. Rising up on my hands and knees, I kissed Joey on the side of his face, then got back into bed feeling much better.

When the doorbell chimed the next morning I was in the kitchen, brushing Joey, a job I was doing for my dad. My mother was in the bathroom, taking a shower. Joey's ears shot up and he looked toward the living room even before the chimes sounded. Then he looked at me as if to say: Let's go see who it is. You don't have to worry because if necessary, I'll attack. I dropped the metal brush to the floor and followed Joey to the living room.

On my knees on the sofa, leaning over the sofa back, I could see most of the front porch through the multi-paned window. No one was there. But Joey, standing in front of the door, kept barking. Between barks he looked at me questioningly: Don't you know someone's out there? Don't you want to find out who it is?

"Nobody's there. Somebody just walked down the sidewalk, or something."

I'd hardly closed my mouth when the person on the porch stepped into my field of vision. Startled, I pulled back, then hopped off the sofa and tore through the living room and down the hall to the bathroom.

My mother had just stepped out of the shower and was reaching for a towel. I blinked at her nakedness, so rarely seen by me and always shocking.

"Mom, come and open the door! Hurry! There's a lady on our porch and she wants to come in!"

"A lady? Oh, I know who it is. Go invite her in while I dry myself and get dressed. Tell her I'll be just a few minutes."

I couldn't. Not in my pajamas. They had feet. I looked like a baby in them. And what I'd left out in telling my mother about the lady on the porch was that she was the most beautiful woman in the world.

"Go on honey, before she goes away. It's the girl who's going to live with the Mooneys. The one I told you about, who can't talk. She moved in this morning, and Mrs. Mooney said she would send her over to meet us. She does odd jobs and might be willing to babysit. Ask her in but keep Joey off her. I'll hurry."

I tromped down the hall to the living room thinking about how silly I looked in my pajamas. Joey wasn't barking anymore, just staring eagerly at the door, which I unlocked and opened while commanding, "Back, Joey!" He cooperated by waggling backwards a few steps.

The girl who was going to live with the Mooneys was carrying a photograph album. It was the same as the one we had on the coffee table in our library, but a different color. She held it with its bottom resting against her stomach. She wore white shorts and a short-sleeved white shirt that was tied at her waist, and all her skin was suntanned. From a gold chain around her neck dangled a small notepad with a green cover. A green pen stuck up from her shirt pocket. She had green eyes with thick lashes, and her short hair fell crookedly over one brow and curled around her ears.

JUST JOEY

It wasn't all one shade, that hair, but most of it was the color of butterscotch pudding that Mrs. Mooney brought over last night as a special treat because I was sick. But what I really noticed about her were her long, sleek, straight, muscular legs. A bruise in the middle of one knee particularly caught my attention. It reminded me that I had an elbow bruise from when Howard Steinberg wrestled me to the floor of his bedroom on the day Alan died.

"Hi," I said. "My mom's getting dressed."

She smiled. I stared. She ducked her head a little, peered in a roundabout way into the living room, and pointed a finger at the interior of the house. Yes, of course. She wanted to come in. I moved out of her way, and she stepped inside. Joey darted forward to get his nose in her crotch. She pushed his face away with one hand, but not in a mean way. Then she dangled her hand in front of Joey's nose. When he'd sniffed the back of it as much as he needed to, she turned it around for him to get the scent of her palm.

"He's an attack dog," I said.

Oh, her eyes said appreciatively. Joey nosed around her bruised knee, then sat down almost at her feet, and grinned up at her. "He bit me once," I said. "There was blood all over."

Her expression, as she reached to wipe her knee dry, showed that she was even more impressed. Then she aimed her attention above and beyond me. I turned and saw my mother.

"Hello, you must be the Mooneys' boarder. I'm so glad to meet you. I'm Tina Frank."

I turned my head again and saw the Mooneys' boarder take a little rectangle of paper from her shirt pocket. She held it out to my mother, who read aloud from it: "Judith Chapman. Bona-fide handyperson. No job too big or too small."

"What a handsome business card! And your name is so distinguished sounding. Are you called Judy, or Judith?"

Judith Chapman set her photo album on the table in front of the sofa, first giving my mother a "May I?" look. I watched with keen interest as she unclipped the little notebook that dangled

24

on her chest from its chain and took out her pen to write. Just as her hand was poised to start writing, she looked down at me and smiled widely, almost mischievously. When she began, I could tell by how her hand and the pen moved that she was printing, not writing. She slipped the pen back into her shirt pocket, then held the piece of paper out to me, not my mom.

Go on, honey, take it," urged my mother. I did, but how I wished she'd give me time to do things on my own before telling me in front of other people to do them!

Judith Chapman had printed, all right, in large capital letters that went straight up and down, north to south as my teacher, Mrs. Levy, would say, except for the west to east line in the middle of H. The two Ps in the center of the word were easily recognized, with their rounded parts looking like balloons on sticks.

"Can you read it?" prompted my mother, peering down over my shoulder.

"C H A P P I E," I spelled out.

"Good, honey. That spells Chappie. Now introduce yourself to Chappie."

I couldn't. The cat had got my tongue, as I'd heard Mrs. Levy say of a boy in first grade who refused to answer a question he was asked.

"This is Gary," my mother said. "Gary Timothy Frank, who is all of six years and five months old. And I'll bet you've met Joey, here, who is eight months old. We got him for Gary's birthday, so we think of him as our birthday puppy."

Fear that she'd tell why I was given a dog for my birthday made all the features on my face freeze. But by the time I'd worried about what my mother would say next, she was already on to another topic. "I think being a handyperson is a very creative career for a woman. You won't find too many females doing that, but they should. Why should men be the only ones who can fix anything?"

After Chappie and my mom had sat down on the sofa to look at the pictures in Chappie's album, I, feeling brave, sat next to

Chappie, but not too close. She moved nearer to me, then opened the album on her lap. Joey plopped down on the carpeted floor next to me, which made me feel important as well as brave.

The photo album had pictures of things Chappie had fixed: damaged roofs, broken sprinkler systems, warped doors. She could fix washing machines and dryers, replace rotted wood, put up shutters or rain gutters. She also replaced old things with new. One picture was a shiny new kitchen floor she'd installed. There was a set of before and after pictures, including a vase broken into ten pieces at least, and the same vase glued back together again.

And Chappie walked dogs. A picture of a jet black dog, that prompted my mother to proclaim that she loved Scotties, was next to a thank you note from the dog's owner. Aloud, my mother read, "If not for you, Chappie, my little Blackie wouldn't have had any exercise while I was recuperating from surgery."

We learned, although there wasn't a picture of this, that Chappie did indeed babysit, for just three dollars an hour, per child. Chappie's notes about sitting, which my mom read aloud, concluded that her work schedule rarely allowed her time to sit during the day.

She was twenty-two. Her people were from Michigan, but she was a native Californian. She didn't belong to the Mooneys' church. She had no family, and had grown up in a 'home'. She'd been to college for a year but quit because she didn't like it. She didn't have a boyfriend. No, she wasn't dating anyone.

I was impressed by my mother's ability to think of so many things to talk about. Sometimes her chattiness irritated me, but not on that day. I would willingly have sat next to Chappie and watched her write the answers to my mother's questions all day long. She didn't print these answers, but luckily my mother read them aloud so I wouldn't be left out. Sometimes Chappie just answered with a facial expression—a nod or shake of her head, hand gestures, or all three. She was able to laugh, I had noticed, even if sound didn't come out of her mouth.

By the time Chappie left, I no longer felt reluctant to go next door to the house of my humiliation. Chappie wanted me to come over when my cold was better, to see her collection of university pennants, and I promised her that I would.

Joey and I tagged after my mother when she walked Chappie to the door. Carrying her album, Chappie turned to smile a silent goodbye, first to my mom, then me, then Joey, and then to my mother again.

I stared at Chappie's knee that had been bruised when she arrived. The black and blue mark had been dark and mean, obviously a new one. Now it was gone. How had that happened? It took a long time for my bruises to go from dark to light and finally fade away to nothing.

After my mother said a final goodbye to Chappie and closed the door, I pulled up my pajama sleeve and crooked my elbow to see if my bruise had faded. It was gone—the same as Chappie's—unless I was looking at the wrong elbow. To find out, I hiked up my other sleeve.

"Are you warm, honey?" asked my mom.

Her voice breaking into my concentration surprised me and made me wary. I didn't want to share with her the mystery of the disappearing bruises. It was something just between me and Chappie, although Chappie didn't know about it.

"Why don't you take off your jammies and get into some clean clothes? You'll feel better. But put on a shirt with long sleeves, so you won't get chilled."

Joey trotted after me to our shared bedroom. After pulling off my pajama top, I double-checked both elbows. Neither showed any sign of injury. Well, I'd sure been wrong about how long black and blue marks lasted. But maybe some kinds went away faster than others. Or maybe as you got older you got better more quickly when you were hurt. There could be a lot of reasons for big ugly bruises vanishing "quick as a wink," as Mrs. Levy would say. Well, whatever had made mine and Chappie's disappear, I didn't know.

"Did you do it, Joey?" I asked. But of course I was only kidding.

CHAPTER 4

He'll Never Be The Same

Overnight Chappie became my special confidant. I told her, and only her, what had happened the night of my birthday. She was sitting for me while my mom was at the dentist's.

"What made the bite on my hand go away?" I asked.

She shrugged.

"Maybe it was because Joey licked my hand. He licked your knee when it had that bruise on it. Then the bruise went away."

She raised her eyebrows.

"Don't you remember? You had a really ugly black and blue mark on your knee the first day you came over. Remember? But when you left you didn't have it. And I saw Joey lick your knee."

She pursed her lips, considering this, then shrugged again. I made a face telling her to think about it. Often, Chappie would answer something I said to her without writing on her notepad, and often I talked to her without speaking.

But from the notes that she did write to me, I was learning to read far ahead of my classmates. That's what my mother said. I also was learning, from being near Chappie and studying her, about feelings unlike any I'd had before. I kept secret the longings that came upon me unexpectedly: to touch her hair or skin, or wrap my arms around her legs the way I did my mother. Only if I were to encircle Chappie's legs, it would be different from hugging my mom. Very different. And I knew I never would do it. In fact, I was careful not to touch Chappie at all.

My mother, sitting at her kitchen desk, telephoned my father in Keystone every night. During one of these conversations I was playing with Joey in the breakfast room, and I overheard my mother say, "I feel so guilty, Lawrence. Gary's cold turned out to be mild, so we could have been there with you."

A pause, then: "No, I couldn't tell. You're right, I know. But honey, I just *really* didn't want to go. I felt I couldn't bear it. I mean, to lose a *child*. Your little boy."

That little boy she was talking about was Alan, and I felt sick to my stomach. I wanted her to hang up. Why did she have to talk about it? And get tears in her eyes all the time over every little thing? Today had been fun but now she'd ruined it, just like she ruined my chance to fly in a plane to South Dakota and see snow. She'd pretended I was getting a bad cold! Why'd she have to do things like that? And how did Howard Steinberg know that snakes eating you didn't hurt if you were dead? I ran to my mother and grabbed her around the waist and ordered, "Get off the phone!" But she already had. I hadn't noticed.

The night before my father returned from South Dakota, my mom read to me from a new book. While leaning into her and staring at the pictures, I made circles on her thigh with my fingertips. "What are you doing?" she asked. "That tickles."

I looked at my fingers on the blue fabric covering her leg, then withdrew my hand and tucked it under my chin. So real had been my feeling that I'd been touching Chappie's bare thigh that my hand seemed to smell of her skin.

My father came home late the next afternoon and the house filled right up again and became brighter. Joey, who was trained not to jump on people, jumped up on him. For one moment that I absolutely loved, Joey rested his paws on his master's chest, and dog and man regarded each other fondly. Then my dad said, "Off, Joey. You know you're not supposed to do that."

"Ellen's doing okay," said my father to my mother at dinner. "It's Ray I'm worried about. This has changed him, Tina. He'll never be the same."

A few minutes later, my mother started telling him about Chappie and what great friends she and I had become. "She's truly inspiring. She always has a happy smile and you never get the feeling that she feels sorry for herself. I don't know what caused her handicap. Mrs. Mooney hasn't said, and it's something you just can't ask. But she can hear perfectly well, for which she must be terribly grateful. So many mute people are also deaf, from the stories I've read. And Chappie's pretty, although she doesn't do a thing for herself. But you couldn't be too particular about your appearance and be in her line of work. Can you imagine, Lawrence, a young handicapped woman without family trying to make her way in the world by doing odd jobs? It's a shame she didn't stay in college. She went for a year. I know she's very bright and could do much better for herself."

I remembered my mother asking Chappie why only men should be able to fix things. Had she forgotten that she'd admired Chappie for being a bona-fide handyperson?

When my mother tucked me into bed that night, I asked, "Don't you think it's good that Chappie can fix things?"

"I certainly do," she said, and her eyes said that she meant it.

"You told Daddy she could do much better for herself."

"Oh, I meant that she could make more money in a job that would earn her more respect. But I couldn't admire her more than I do. You heard me tell Daddy she was an inspiration, and she is."

That satisfied me. But there was something else I wanted to talk about. I'd forgotten it before, but had just now remembered. "Why won't Uncle Ray ever be the same?"

Her eyes filled, making me sorry I'd asked. "It's because of his loss."

In the semi-dark, after she'd left the room, I imagined my uncle coming to visit us and looking like a totally different person. He'd be a stranger, who spoke with a stranger's voice.

I hoped nothing would ever make me change, or my mom or dad, or Chappie. I knew for certain that Joey wouldn't change.

I was nine and Christmas was right around the corner, according to my fourth grade teacher, Miss Shigenaga, when Joey had his second seizure. It was a Friday afternoon. I was walking home from school. My mother, home alone with Joey, witnessed the convulsion, which lasted about half a minute. When I walked in the front door Joey came to greet me, but his expression was different, and his eyes seemed not to focus on mine. Instead of following me to the kitchen, he wandered away, unsteady on his feet.

In the kitchen, my mother was on the phone with the veterinary clinic. Hearing her part of the conversation, I understood what had happened.

We took Joey to the clinic. Two ladies were in the waiting room when we arrived, each with a dog at her feet. After she'd signed in at the reception counter, my mother said to the lady with the fuzzy brown puppy, "My, how darling," and to the other woman, "What a beautiful Lab."

Both ladies complimented Joey in turn. Their dogs were getting vaccinations. When my mom explained why we were there, I knelt by Joey and wrapped an arm around him protectively.

In the examining room, Dr. Meiners, a man with a soft voice and no smile, said that a dog with a convulsive disorder could live out its normal lifespan. "That's another six or seven years in Joey's case. The danger is if he has a seizure cluster. That's three or more in a twenty-four hour period. A cluster can cause brain damage, or even result in the dog's death. But we're miles and miles away from that with Joey, and hopefully we'll never come to it. What we want to do now is put him on medication that will control the problem, at least to a degree."

Dr. Meiners had lots more to say in his droning voice. He stroked Joey's head and back continuously while talking. Whenever I thought he was through talking, and we could leave, my mom asked another question and the doctor answered it at length. When at last a helper came in to lift Joey off the examining table, and we returned to the waiting room, it was full. With so many people and pets crowded into the small space, there wasn't a spare chair and you could hardly see the reception counter.

While my mother stood in line to pay, I held Joey's leash. He kept looking around the room. He was tense—nervous. Holding tight to the lead, I hoped Joey wasn't going to have another seizure. That would be two within twenty-four hours. It was horrifying to think that he really could have a seizure cluster and be brain damaged or die.

Suddenly Joey darted forward, pulling me with him. My mother would later describe what happened next as "Joey's rampage." He ran around the room licking animals. He jumped up on people to get to the animals in their arms. He licked a terrier, a spaniel, a chow chow, another shepherd, and some kind of growly, long-legged, hard-eyed dog wearing a muzzle. He tried to stick his tongue through an air hole in a cat carrier. A parrot's beak poked through a hole in another carrier made of cardboard, and Joey licked the beak. Then he went for an Irish setter just coming through the glass doors. I kept meaning to shout "Off!" but was so busy trying to control Joey that I never did.

A bent-over blue-haired woman came through the doors with a small white poodle in her arms, and Joey lunged. Shouts of alarm went up as the woman fell over sideways and the poodle tumbled from her arms. "My ankle," groaned the woman after she hit the floor. Then: "Bitsy? Where's my Bitsy?"

I had seen the poodle scurry to hide under a chair, behind a man's legs. I hadn't noticed my mother take Joey's lead from me. But she couldn't restrain him. He tugged against the lead so hard that he managed to close the distance between himself and the fallen woman. He licked her ankle.

A man shouted, "That dog's a menace! It should be put down!"

As soon as the man had spoken, Joey became perfectly calm. No more pulling. No more licking. "Take him to the car," my mother said, her voice trembling. Her hands shook when she gave me the lead, and when I started walking, my knees wobbled.

The man who wanted Joey dead had helped Bitsy's owner up from the floor, and the young woman with the parrot in a box had given up her chair for her. The last words I heard as I led Joey outside were, "My ankle's fine now, and so is Bitsy's paw. Look, her limp is gone."

Later that afternoon, lying under my favorite tree in the backyard, with Joey asleep beside me, I worried that he would be taken away. All my mom had said about what happened at Dr. Meiners was that she would have to talk to my father about it, but not until late that night.

They were going to a dinner dance that night, to celebrate the fiftieth wedding anniversary of a teacher who used to work at my dad's high school. "I don't want to ruin the evening for Daddy," my mother said on our way home from the clinic. Joey was sound asleep in the back. "I'll tell him after the party or tomorrow morning. But Gary, listen, because this is very important. If Joey has a seizure while we're out, you call us immediately. And don't get near him. Don't let Jennifer near him either. He could bite someone accidentally."

Like he bit me the first day we had him, I thought, but didn't say anything.

"We probably shouldn't go out tonight. I know we shouldn't. But this party's so special. I know the Halls would be disappointed if your father wasn't there. Mr. Hall and Daddy just have this tremendous respect for each other."

Lying under the tree, I closed my eyes and remembered Joey's rampage. Joey hadn't hurt anyone or any pet, but still he shouldn't have done what he did. I had to grin, though, when I remembered the looks on some of those people's faces.

I had fallen asleep beneath the tree. When I wakened a while later, it took a moment before I remembered what had happened. I sat up and looked around for Joey.

His hindquarters were sticking out from under the largest shrub in the yard. Curious because I hadn't seen Joey pay attention to that shrub before, not even to lift his leg on it, I got up and went to see what had his interest. Gently, I pulled him out from the plant, then crawled under it.

I found myself eye to eye with a mourning dove that quite obviously had a broken wing. My stomach knotted. Was it the mother dove that nested in the tree outside my bedroom window last summer, or one of her babies?

I didn't know if I should scoop up the injured bird with my bare hands or go inside to get a soft towel—and my mom. While I was deciding, Joey darted under the shrub again. He pushed in front of me. I couldn't see the dove or what was going on. I backed out from the plant, and pulled Joey with me. "You better not have killed it," I cried.

He turned and looked at me quizzically. I knew I had to crawl under the shrub to see if the bird was still alive, but I sure didn't want to. This was really a job for my mother, not me, except that I didn't want her to know Joey had done something else bad. I felt wretched. "Why didn't you leave it alone?" I asked Joey angrily.

Just then the dove strutted out, unhurt, her damaged wing healed. She hurried past me with a look that said she didn't need me or trust me, then flew away.

I went to bed that Friday night happier than I'd ever been. I'd been thinking ceaselessly about the poodle's paw, the woman's ankle, the bird's wing, my own hand when I was six, and the bruises that disappeared from my elbow and from Chappie's knee the day we met.

Joey made sick things become well by licking them. He really and truly did. That's why he'd had his rampage. And that letter from Uncle Ray that my mother had left on her kitchen desk, and Joey had taken and licked all over? He'd been trying to make Alan well! If only we'd taken Joey to South Dakota before Alan died, he *wouldn't* have died.

In the morning I would explain all this to my parents, then go next door and tell Chappie. I was itching to talk about it now, but Jennifer, the babysitter, was never interested in anything I said. What a rotten deal that Chappie couldn't sit for me tonight because she'd had to go to a dumb baby shower for her girl-friend. She'd have been interested. My parents, though, probably wouldn't believe me at first. For proof, I might have to cut my hand and make it bleed, and then have Joey make the cut get well by licking my hand.

Because I had no one to talk to, I got out of bed and stretched out on the floor next to Joey. Joey, the magic dog, who with a lick of the tongue made people and animals and even birds with broken wings get well.

I woke in the morning to find myself all alone on the floor with Joey's blanket pulled over me. Voices, both male and female, came from the living room. Had someone come over? I didn't hear either my mother's or father's voice.

I walked down the hall and stood in the entrance to the living room. Jennifer was still here, for some reason, and her parents had come over, which was entirely strange. The other people were Mr. and Mrs. Mooney, Chappie, and a policeman. They were all sitting down, with Joey next to the cop. When they saw me, they stopped talking and stared, except for Mr. and Mrs. Mooney, who quickly looked down at their laps.

Joey stood and trotted up to me and gave me a few nibble kisses.

Chappie and the policeman stood up at the same time. When Chappie crossed in front of him to get to me, the police-man said, "Uh, excuse me."

Chappie stood at my side, looking with me toward the oth-ers. Her hand found mine. We had never held hands before.

The cop said, "Hi, Gary. I'm Mike. Son, your parents have been in an accident. They're in the hospital. Your dad's fine. They're just going to keep him there to watch him for a little while. But your mother—well, she's pretty badly hurt."

CHAPTER 5

Strength

Mrs. Mooney stiffly rose to her feet, aided by her husband and a cane. The curve of her body made the ends of her buttonless sweater fall forward. When Mr. Mooney let go of her hand, I thought that without the cane she could crash right down onto the coffee table.

"I'm going to go home and make breakfast for you, Gary, dear," she said. "I'll be back with it in just a little while."

Mr. Mooney followed her from the living room. At the door, he turned to admonish me not to "go eating a bowl of cereal or getting into the cookie jar." His tone became conspiratorial as he explained, "When Mrs. Mooney says she's going to make breakfast for you, Gary, you'd best prepare yourself for a feast."

"I believe *that*," chuckled Mike the cop, who was the next to leave after the Mooneys.

"Well," said Jennifer's mother. "I suppose . . . if you're staying, Chappie?"

Chappie was still holding my hand. She nodded, and Jennifer and her parents rose to their feet at once. Smiling a sad smile, the babysitter's mother came to me and to my great dismay bent to kiss my cheek. This was uncalled for! I let go of Chappie's hand, embarrassed at having her witness the kiss.

When only Chappie remained in the house with Joey and me, I went to my room to dress. I chose clothes that I didn't like but my mother did. When I'd finished tying the laces of my good shoes, I stood in front of the mirror on the closet door to comb my hair. Turning my head from side to side to check how I looked, I discovered lipstick. *Yuck! Vomit!* Red as blood, it was almost touching my right ear, and I imagined it sliding in and staining my brain. I dropped the comb, snatched up my pajama top from the floor, and roughly rubbed the stuff away. Now my hair on that side was all messed up, so I dropped the pajama top, retrieved the comb, and repaired the damage. Miss Shigenaga, my fourth grade teacher, always said to the class before special event days, "Tomorrow will not be a day for looking sloppy, boys and girls." I told myself that when your parents had been in an accident and were in the hospital, and your mother was hurt real bad, it was not a day for looking sloppy.

Still looking in the mirror, I noticed Joey watching me. He was sitting quietly, doing nothing but gazing sorrowfully at the boy he loved. People always said that Joey's eyes were sorrowful, or mournful. And it was true that Joey's mostly-black face usually did wear a sad expression, especially when people outside his own family were around.

But when he was with those whom he loved—my mom, dad, and me, and to a lesser degree Chappie—Joey usually looked happy. When I came home from school, for instance, or my father came home from the high school where he taught science, Joey's mouth widened into a big happy grin. He also looked happy when he followed my mother around the house, or sat and listened to her talk to him while she worked in her flower gardens.

I turned from the mirror and dropped to my knees in front of Joey and put my arms around his thick, thick neck. That strong-as-steel neck was always a reassurance, as was the identity tag suspended from his collar.

I clasped the tag in one hand. It had JOEY printed on one side, with our phone number. The other side read LAWRENCE FRANK and gave our address. Always, the words on that round piece of metal satisfied me that my father's protection was a blanket over Joey just as it was a blanket over me and my mother.

And Joey protected us, too. This German shepherd with the big black ears and white-haired belly and long, black-tipped tail was *so strong*. Joey's strength was that of a wrestler, a grizzly bear, Superman.

You'll make her well, won't you boy? You'll make my mother well for me. Dad can't. He can protect us from robbers and killers but not sickness and car crashes. But you can do it, Joey. You'll just lick her and she'll be well again.

I got up. Joey also rose to a standing position. The morning sun, pouring through the window behind me, turned to gold the smooth tan hair above Joey's brow, and also the rough, thick fur on his sturdy chest. This was not only the strongest and smartest and most special dog in the world, I knew, but the best-looking, too. My mother often claimed that Joey could be a show dog, he was so handsome.

Tears burned in my eyes. I leaned over to hug Joey again, this time burying my face in the fur on the back of his neck. It was there—in a band between his part-black and part-tan head, and his part-black and part-tan back—that his many colors combined. Mixed together these shades of black, tan, gold, cream, and white made no color that I knew but were just Joey. I wiped my tears on that neck fur and vowed not to cry again for as long as I lived.

Mrs. Mooney had sent Mr. Mooney over with my breakfast on a tray that was round and white as the moon itself. When I entered the breakfast room, he said, "Here you are, son. Come and sit yourself down while this is all still warm."

I stared as he placed on the table a plate filled to overflowing with three waffles, one fried egg, and four strips of bacon. Two pats of butter were melting over the top waffle.

I sat. My mom never made breakfasts like this. "This is a feast," I announced, followed by, "I need syrup."

Mr. Mooney said, "Ah, let's see, where does your . . . what cupboard will I find it in?" His pink face darkened as he spoke.

Chappie took over for Mr. Mooney, bringing me the syrup, a knife, fork, and napkin, and glasses of orange juice and milk.

Mr. Mooney seemed unsure whether to stay or leave. Finally, he patted me on the shoulder, said, "Enjoy your breakfast, son," and left.

Chappie sat down across from me and without my permission snitched the crispest piece of bacon from my plate. Since the bacon was closest to her, I turned the plate so it wouldn't be. Bacon was my favorite breakfast food, but we seldom had it because, as my mother said, three people eating as much bacon as they want to eat is a very expensive proposition—especially on a teacher's salary. I would save one piece to eat last, as if it were a dessert.

"I could hardly wait for Mr. Mooney to leave," I told Chappie while reaching for the orange juice.

She gave me her "How come?" look.

I drank, then set the glass down. "Cause. I'll tell you in a minute. I just want to eat some waffle first." Actually, I was worried that Chappie wouldn't go along with my plan to take Joey to the hospital.

Joey lay with his front half under the table, which he rarely did anymore. While I carefully cut my egg to separate the white from the yolk, I imagined how it would be when Joey made my mother well. It was going to be something to see when a giant police dog ran up to a woman with bones broken and stuff, and with just a few licks of his big slurpy tongue made her so much better that she could leave the hospital first thing the next morning. The hospital people would want to keep her there tonight, I supposed, to watch her, and that was okay. She could use a good rest in the hospital after so much excitement. But my father wouldn't need watching anymore. He'd leave the hospital right away, with me and Joey and Chappie.

As I poured more syrup around the edges of a waffle, I pictured the hospital doctors and nurses, lined up at either side of a long hallway. They'd be cheering and clapping as my dad and I, with our magic dog that cured people, and with our beautiful neighbor, strode down that hall and right out the hospital door.

Chappie leaned forward and touched her fingertips to the knuckles of my left hand, which lay resting on the table. If my mother had been home she'd have told me, without scolding, to keep the hand in my lap while eating. But Chappie didn't care about such things. I looked up from my plate and met her eyes, which I liked better than any other eyes in the world except Joey's. Chappie's eyes never lied, never showed embarrassment, never looked at me in a way that made me feel dumb.

She tapped her butterscotch hair with one finger, then pointed the finger at my head, then used the finger to draw a question mark in the air between us.

"I'm thinking about Joey making my mom and dad well, especially my mom," I answered. "He can. See, yesterday . . ."

I told her about the rampage, and about the dove. I reminded her that Joey had bitten me the first night we had him, and that the wound had disappeared after Joey licked my hand. I spoke softly, as if someone who might want to thwart my plan lurked somewhere in the house, I said, "We have to take Joey to the hospital right after I finish my breakfast."

Under the table, Joey whimpered. My fist froze around my fork and my mouth closed over the shame in my throat. Here I was, eating enough breakfast for an army, and Joey hadn't had anything to eat. My mother was the one who put Joey's food out in the morning, and changed the water in his bowl. "I have to feed him and change his water," I said, getting up from the table. "I forgot."

Then I remembered the bottle of pills that my mother had placed on the kitchen counter when we got back from Dr. Meiners' yesterday. Joey was supposed to be given two pills in the morning and two at night, to keep him from having a seizure. My having forgotten this part of his care, even temporarily, was too embarrassing a mistake to admit to Chappie. "You can have my last piece of bacon if you want," I told her instead.

While Chappie ate bacon, I crouched on the floor in front of Joey to make sure that the pills went in with the food. I had always liked watching Joey eat, because he did it lying flat on his stomach with the bowl between his front paws. My parents had both said that they'd never seen another dog eat that way.

Chappie tapped me on the shoulder, and I looked up. She handed me two pieces of her notepaper, each written on both sides. The entire message read: "We can't take Joey inside a hospital. It's against rules. We'd be in big trouble. Besides, he'd go on a rampage the way he did yesterday. He'd be running all over the place trying to cure people. We wouldn't be able to control him and anything could happen. Horrible things. He could frighten a patient into having a heart attack. He could make a surgeon's knife slip. Can you imagine if a person was having his appendix taken out, and a huge dog jumped on the doctor and he cut right through the patient's liver or kidney? Gary, that woman Joey knocked over at the vet's was lucky her skull didn't split in two. I'm not kidding. And I'm telling you we can't do it."

I surprised myself by how fast I sprang to my feet, and the way Chappie's eyes widened showed that she too was surprised.

Chappie was tall—taller than my mom, anyway, and I was still short. She'd had her twenty-fifth birthday, whereas I'd just had my ninth. But as authoritatively as I could, I said, "We have to do it. I'll do it by myself if you won't go with me. But if we both do it, I know we can control him."

She mouthed, "How?"

The answer came to me in a flash. "Joey has an extra leash. If we each hold one of them, we can keep him between us, and that way we can control him. It'll be a cinch, Chappie. Come on. *Please?*"

After having regarded me a long moment, she raised a hand between us and pantomimed shaking keys on a chain.

Victory! I almost hugged her—but caught myself in time. Pretending to shake car keys was Chappie's way of saying, "Let's go."

Chappie's two-tone green Chevy had four doors but no back seat. She'd taken it out to make room for the things a bona-fide handyperson needed in her work. Joey rode standing beside a busted cane-backed chair that hadn't been repaired yet. Sitting in front with Chappie, I was glad the chair was there to keep Joey from being thrown against the wall of the car and hurting himself if Chappie had to slam on the brakes.

When I realized that we weren't driving to Community Hospital, I asked, "Where are we going? Aren't my parents at Community?"

She shook her head no.

"But that's where we go," I protested. "I was born there and when Joey bit me my mom took me there."

Chappie turned toward me with her "I can't talk now" look. She didn't enjoy conversations while she was driving, and who could blame her? I kept quiet, but this unexpected twist of my parents not being at Community Hospital troubled me. Community was what I was familiar with, and I'd formed a mental image of my parents there: my dad sitting up in a hospital bed, eating food from a tray over his lap and watching television; my mom in the emergency room, on a bed or a table, with bright lights overhead and doctors and nurses forming a half circle around her. For some reason, I felt unable to transfer these images to another, unknown hospital. Now I felt far away from my parents, and it was more than distance that separated me from them.

The hospital we drove to was much bigger and more modern than Community, and it faced a busy, wide, flat boulevard. Community was perched on a hilly street with houses that had flower gardens in front, and cars went by it slowly. I felt confirmed in my apprehension.

When Chappie pulled into the parking lot, I turned so I could see Joey's reaction to being so near sick people. His expression, as he peered through the side window, was certainly alert, but he didn't seem excited. "I don't think he knows he's near sick people," I said.

Chappie gave me a look that said, "He will soon."

"How're we going to get him in the building?" I asked, having lost the confidence I'd felt at home.

She slipped her pen out of her shirt pocket and unclipped her notepad from its chain. I hoped for a short note. It could wear my patience down, waiting for her to finish writing, and of course I could never show that I minded it at all.

When she gave me the note I silently read, "We'll find a side door and you'll wait there with Joey. I'll go in the main entrance. I'll find out where your mom is and go there first, then come and let you in. That way we'll know where we're—"

She snatched the two sheets of paper from my fingers, wadded them up in a ball, and threw it down by her feet.

"What'd you do that for?" I demanded "I wasn't finished."

She shook her head vigorously.

"Why not? It'll work! We just have to get Joey to her room without anyone seeing us. What's so hard about that?"

I knew, though, that everything about it would be hard. Hallways in hospitals probably weren't ever empty. Nurses constantly went from room to room to check on people to see if they were breathing and if they needed a shot for their pain. Visitors brought flowers and candy to the patients. Suddenly I had a great idea. "If someone sees us we'll pretend Joey's a seeing-eye dog. You'll walk with your eyes closed and act like you're blind. I'll hold your hand. It'll look like I'm helping Joey lead you. We'll just be visitors going to see someone like everybody else. Only we'll have a seeing-eye dog with us."

As easily as that idea had come to me, another one did. "Or we can do something like I saw once in a movie where these two really crazy guys snuck another guy into a police station to help another one who'd robbed a bank get out. See—we'll take Joey in through a door nobody uses and real fast hide him somewhere, and then—"

It shocked me when she pressed her fingers to my mouth to silence me. She'd never done that before. I didn't like it at all. But when she took her hand away to begin writing again, I didn't say a word. Chappie's writing was the same as another person's speaking. I knew she hated it when someone interrupted her by talking at the same time she did.

Joey, who hadn't made a sound while we talked, now yawned noisily. I turned around until I was on my knees, then reached across the seat back to pet him. It was strange that Joey was so calm, I thought. Usually, when something important was going to happen, he suspected it and got real excited.

It was even more strange that my mother had no idea that we were out here in the parking lot, planning to make her well.

I turned on the seat, sat back down, and felt less nervous than I'd been. Chappie's idea was going to be better than either of mine, both of which had been pretty dumb, I now realized. I mean, come on. Seeing Joey walking with Chappie, who would believe that she was blind. She didn't have a white cane with a red tip, and Joey didn't have one of those special harnesses for seeing-eye dogs. And my other idea had been worse. Get Joey into one of those laundry bags that are carried on a cart, and get him to stay still inside it while we wheeled him to the room my mother was in? Never! It wouldn't have worked.

I'd been staring out the window while trying to come up with another idea, when Chappie nudged my arm and I turned to look at her. She held out the note that had taken her practically forever to write. I grabbed the sheets of paper, and, because of the number of syllables in some of the words, read at a wildly uneven speed:

"You'll go in through the front while I wait outside with Joey. You'll tell the person at the reception desk that you need to see either a hospital administrator or your mother's doctor. Tell her your mom's name and explain that she's the woman who was critically injured in a car accident last night. When someone with authority comes to talk to you, say that your mother loves her dog more than anything in the world. Say he's an extremely well-behaved German shepherd who is waiting outside with an adult friend who will be responsible for his behavior in the hospital. Say that your mother loves her dog so much that seeing him could have miraculous results for her. Say that she's always said that an animal's love is so perfect an expression of God's grace that it can heal any hurt. Say she really believes that with all her heart. Say it convincingly, Gary. You have to say it as if you do believe you've heard those exact words come from her. Then say that you're afraid your mother might die from her injuries and you want to help her, and bringing Joey to her is the only way you know how. Say something like she loves him so much, and if she feels better after seeing him, I'll know I've helped her. But if I don't bring him to her, then I'll know I let her down.

My breath had stopped in my throat when I read the words about my mother possibly dying from her injuries. She couldn't! I needed her. My dad did, too. And Joey did. All three of us needed her—and loved her.

When I was finished reading, Chappie held another piece of paper in front of my face. On it she had written, "Do you think you can do it?"

"Yes," I answered, but my voice sounded as uncertain as I felt.

She began writing again, her head bent in concentration over the notepad, which had grown thinner. When she was done I read, "If they say no to you, there's something else you can try. Ask very politely if you may see your father. They should let you do that. Then ask your dad to get them to let us bring Joey in."

"But my dad doesn't know Joey has magic powers! What if he doesn't think it's true? I'll bet he won't because he never saw anything I saw. He didn't go with us to the vet's yesterday. He didn't see the dove. And when Joey bit me the night we got him and the bite went away, he said our eyes played tricks on us. He doesn't even know about the black and blue marks that went away. Not even that! He doesn't know *any* of it!"

Chappie sighed, staring hard at me. Then she started writing again. The note said: "I hope you can convince someone who's able to help you that seeing Joey would be the most wonderful thing for your mother. It's a long shot, Gary, but if there are kind people inside this hospital, and if they feel sorry enough for you, they just might let you bring him in."

I'd scarcely finished reading this before Chappie opened the door on her side and got out. With perspiring hands, I searched through the notes on my lap to find the one with the things I was supposed to say. Having read it again, I tried practicing the words without looking at them. I got as far as "perfect."

Joey was wriggling and whining. He always got excited before being let into or out of a car. I turned and saw Chappie attach the second lead to his collar. His whimpering became louder. My heart raced.

"Come on," Chappie mouthed at me across the seat back.

Once more I read the words I was to say inside the hospital, then opened the door and got out. Diamonds of light leapt up from the pavement to blind me.

Perfect expression of God's love. God's grace. Perfect expression of God's grace. It can heal anything. Any hurt. God's grace. God's grace.

I had to hurry to keep up with Chappie.

Please sir, I'm afraid that my mother . . . I'm afraid that my mother might die. I'm afraid that my mother might die of her injuries.

Chappie's fingers touched my arm. I stopped walking and looked up. We were in front of the main entrance to the hospital. I stared at the glass doors. Then I turned to look at Chappie. Her face had become oddly white. I looked for Joey but didn't see him. A second later, my eyes found him standing next to Chappie, on her left. But in that moment of not knowing where he was, I'd felt terror, and I could not do what Chappie wanted. "I can't do it," I whispered. "I can't go in there alone, Chappie."

She stepped behind Joey, which put him on her right, then handed me the grips of the leashes. In one easy motion she pointed first toward a very low wall in front of some plants, then at me, then at Joey, and again at the wall.

I walked to the wall. When I turned around in front of it, Chappie had disappeared into the building. I sat down to wait. Joey was staring at the hospital doors. "Joey, sit," I said. He remained standing. He even took a few steps forward. He kept his ears straight up and his mouth tightly closed. He never looked away from the doors. "Joey, sit," I said again. Again he didn't obey, but he didn't strain at the lead, either. He was being good. It didn't matter so much if he ignored the sit command.

"Nice dog," said a man who came out of the building and walked past us. Joey didn't look up. He just watched the hospital doors. Did he know why we'd come here, I wondered. Was he waiting to be taken inside, or was he just waiting for Chappie to come back?

No matter how well you know a dog, a lot of the time you don't know what's going on in his head. I had been imagining myself sharing this thought with my parents when we were home together again, when Chappie came out of the building. Joey nearly dragged me to her. I asked, "What'd they say?" Giving no answer except an angry shake of her head, she kept walking. Sometimes Chappie walked so fast that her long legs, bare and gleaming below her shorts, made me think of a shark gobbling up the ground under them. This was such a time.

I hurried after her, angry myself. I'd seen that her cheeks were red and her mouth bunched up tight. I could imagine what had happened. "Are you crazy?" the hospital administrator or my mother's doctor had asked after reading Chappie's note. People would have gathered around by then, making it more embarrassing for her. "Are you some kind of a nut? You want to bring a dog in here to lick a woman who's been hurt so bad she's practically dead?"

Chappie wouldn't have bothered writing another note. How do you change someone's mind about you once he's decided you're stupid or crazy? The person she'd given her note to must have thought that the *real* loony was Tina Frank—believing that stuff about an animal's love and God's perfect grace, whatever that meant.

I felt angrier by the second. Here we were with Joey, who could make my mother well, and those dumb jerks in the hospital wouldn't let him inside to do it!

Reaching the Chevy, Chappie yanked open the door on the driver's side, then opened the rear door for Joey. He wanted to get inside but Chappie held him back so she could detach the second lead from his collar. While she did this, I looked at the broken chair and thought that my mother, too, was broken.

I didn't let Joey get in the car. Gripping his lead, I turned and ran back to the hospital entrance and pushed the door open and pulled Joey inside and shouted across the room to the lady behind the reception desk: "I want to see Mrs. Frank! She's my Mother! Where is she?"

CHAPTER 6

The Deal

The yellow-haired woman sitting behind the desk slid her glasses down her nose and peered at Joey and me. She slid them back up and came around the desk straight at us. Not before I could see the wrinkles that cut into her doughy face did she stop.

"Take that dog outside instantly, young man! I told the mute girl it couldn't come inside. This is a hospital!"

"I have to see my mother," I said.

"Not with that dog!" She cupped her hands in front of her ample bosom and clapped them together once, making a hollow sound. "Out!" Her smoldering glare went from me to Joey and back to me before she barked, "Now! Immediately!"

At "Immediately," Joey slunk into an unhappy "down"—his ears laid back and snout cradled between his paws.

I said to the woman, "His name's Joey. He's housebroken and he doesn't bite. May I please take him to see my mother, just for a second?"

She couldn't have looked more offended if I'd said that as soon as Joey's stools fall to the lawn flies settled on them.

"You may not," she said. "And if you don't take him outside immediately, I'll get someone who will."

"But my mother was in a car crash and she's hurt real bad and Joey can make her better. Please? He'll just lick her. Then I'll take him outside."

She opened her mouth but whatever she intended to say never came out. "Pat?" asked the voice of another lady, from behind the one who had me so frustrated and Joey so frightened. Tiny green and red Christmas tree ornaments dangled from her ears. "Patty? What's wrong? Oh! Oh, my goodness."

You only had to hear the way she said "goodness" to know she liked dogs. I blurted, "My mother's Mrs. Frank who was in a car crash last night. I have to take my dog to see her! He won't do anything bad, and he'll make her so much better it will be a miracle. A miraculous result! God's perfect grace! And my friend Chappie who's grown up is waiting in the parking lot and she'll take responsibility for Joey while he's in here. My dad's here too. Mr. Frank. He's a science teacher. He was in the accident with my mom and he's being watched. Will you let me take Joey to see my mother? It'll help her! Please!"

And once more, though I was out of breath and trembling, I begged *please.*

"His friend's a mute girl who does odd jobs," said the mean lady. "I have her business card."

The nice one ignored this. She knelt on the floor in front of Joey and gave him the back of her hand to smell.

But Joey didn't sniff her hand. He didn't raise his head even an inch off the floor. It was as if the other woman's dislike of him had broken his heart.

"Well, Joey," the friendly one said. "Aren't you a good dog? Yes, you are, and so handsome." She rose to her feet. "And what's *your* name?" she asked. Her smile said that once she knew my name we would be the best of friends.

"Gary Timothy Frank," I answered, hoping that three names would make me seem an even better citizen.

"Hello, Gary. I'm Mrs. Stead. I'm not authorized to allow a dog inside the hospital, but I'll see if I can't find someone to talk to you about it. Why don't you take Joey outside to your friend, Chappie. Is she taking care of you while your parents are here?"

"Yes," I answered, and along with the realization that she was taking care of me, came hope. How can you not believe that all will turn out well when a person with more wisdom, experience, and courage than you have is taking care of you?

"Well, that's fine," said Mrs. Stead. "So you take Joey outside and leave him with Chappie, then come back. Mrs. Carlson will bring you to my office."

Very briefly, Mrs. Stead turned toward the meanie, whose features were now molded into civility.

"Do you think the person you find to help me will let me bring Joey in to see my mother?" I asked this believing that the answer would be yes. "Would you ask for me?"

"I will, Gary. But I really can't promise you anything." Mrs. Stead's voice and expression had become serious, almost sad. "You see, dear, animals aren't permitted to visit their owners in hospitals because of the germs they carry. It's very important for your mother not to be exposed to germs just now. Protecting her from germs is one of the ways the doctors and nurses are helping her."

Smiling as if the matter of germs, having been discussed, no longer concerned us much, Mrs. Stead said, "But you take Joey out to Chappie, and I'll see what I can do. I'm certain that at the very least we'll be able to get you in to see your father. You'd like that, wouldn't you?"

"Yes," I replied. And as if being prompted by my mom, I added, "Thank you."

I'd wanted to say to Mrs. Stead that my father had told me that a dog's mouth is cleaner than people's mouths, but I hadn't done it at the right moment and now it seemed too late. I looked down at Joey, who hadn't moved yet, no doubt because Mrs. Carlson hadn't gone back to her desk. "Joey, stand," I said, although this command wasn't one he was good at.

He surprised me by getting right to his feet. "Goodbye, Joey," smiled Mrs. Stead.

"I'll be right back," I said.

In sugary, jingly tones Mrs. Carlson said, "I'll be waiting for you."

I hurried outside with Joey to tell Chappie everything that had happened. She was in the car with her arms and face resting on the steering wheel. Her window was all the way down. When I called, "Chappie!" her head bobbed up and she stared at me with shiny eyes. I opened the door for Joey and he got in. He was panting now, as if all the excitement of the last minutes had finally caught up with him. After closing the door, I told my story to Chappie through her window. When I finished, she leaned across the front seat and opened the passenger door.

"But I'm going back inside," I said.

She pointed a finger at me, then at the car seat next to her.

"But I have to go back. Mrs. Stead is waiting for me!"

She unclipped her notepad. Of all times for her to write one of her damn notes. But of course I couldn't complain about it.

The note read, "Tell me again what she said about taking animals into hospitals. Tell me exactly what she said. Don't leave anything out."

"She said . . . she said—"

Chappie nodded. The nod meant: "See?"

I did see. I saw that I'd failed. I should have told Mrs. Stead what happened at Dr. Meiners' and about Joey making the dove well. I should have told her what my dad said about dogs' mouths being cleaner than people's mouths.

But would it have made a difference? I thought not. Even if Mrs. Stead had believed me about Joey, and even if she was willing to repeat such a wild-sounding story to someone who had the authority she lacked, Joey wouldn't be allowed to see my mother. I could go back inside, but not Joey, and I would only hear someone else tell me what Mrs. Stead already had.

I walked around the front of the car and got in and slammed the door shut. Chappie reached out a hand, firmly took hold of my chin, and turned my face toward her. I expected her to mouth, "Don't slam the door!"

She didn't mouth anything. We just looked at each other a long moment before she let go and turned away from me and turned the key in the ignition. I'd seen that she'd been crying while Joey and I were inside the building. Even so, her eyes shone pure grass-green, the color of our lawn when my father would say to my mother words such as: "Now I've got it the way I want it, Tina. If only I could get it to stay this way all the time."

Before Chappie pulled into the Mooneys' driveway, I saw my father standing in front of our house. Excitement filled me when I considered that his being home might mean that Mrs. Stead had spoken to him, and he'd come for Joey and me to take us to my mother.

But it was also possible that the hospital doctors had decided he didn't need watching anymore and had sent him home where, where he'd stood outside a long time worrying about me—not knowing where I was and thinking that I too had been in an accident. Thinking perhaps that I'd been killed.

Or maybe he'd been waiting out on the lawn because he was mad as hell at me.

I walked from the Mooneys' driveway to where my father waited, but Joey ran to him and jumped on him. My father pushed him off, but without giving the "Off!" command, even when Joey leapt up a second and third time. He didn't say anything to Joey, or to me. He had a thick bandage on his forehead, which of course was why Joey had needed to keep jumping on him until he'd gotten a lick in.

I had many emotions while facing my father on our front lawn, and they included shyness brought on by something I saw in his expression. His mouth was closed tight and he kept shifting his eyes away from me, but he looked wide open, with all his hurt showing. It seemed that if I spoke to him, or touched him, he might crumple to the ground and start bawling.

I grabbed the lead Joey was dragging behind himself as he went around my dad, sniffing at his legs. "Sit, Joey," I said. He obeyed. Getting up the courage to talk to my dad, I asked, "Did Mrs. Stead talk to you?"

"Who?"

"The lady at the hospital. Chappie took me and Joey there. I wanted to see Mom, but I didn't get to. Mrs. Stead said—"

"You can't see her, Gary."

Abruptly, he got down on his knees. My stomach flip-flopped in fear that he would cry. "Come here," he said harshly, opening his arms to me. Timidly, I hugged him. He held me tight. Joey licked his forehead again.

"Joey has to see her," I said. Then I told him everything.

His response came in a hoarse whisper. "Gary . . . son, what you think . . . what you want to believe . . . simply isn't so. Joey can't . . . he doesn't have healing powers."

I pulled away and demanded, "How do you know he doesn't? Chappie believes it! You can ask her if you want!"

I'd never in my life talked back to him. My mother, yes, and often, but not him. I turned around to face the Mooneys' house, partly to see if Chappie was still outside, but mostly to avoid my father's eyes.

Chappie had gone inside.

My father rose to his feet and said to me, "Wait in the car with Joey. I'll get my keys."

We didn't talk in the car. We hardly looked at each other. He did pat my knee once.

When we entered the hospital parking lot I asked, "Why didn't you go to Community Hospital?"

"I—"

That was all. I didn't pursue it. It was starting to seem as if some dark thing were being kept from me.

Before opening his door, my father said that I should wait in the car with Joey. This was a disappointment. I'd thought all three of us would march right in and go see my mother. I'd thought nobody could tell Lawrence Frank that he couldn't do something once he'd made up his mind to do it.

Watching him walk away, I lost that faith. He looked old. Before, in front of our house, he'd looked like a sad little boy. Not now. He seemed an old man. His shoulders curved forward; his arms didn't swing at his sides. The tension in me threatened to explode. I twisted on my seat to look at Joey in back and almost shouted at him. "Dad will be okay when Mom's well. You'll see. He won't be changed at all."

During the long wait I had to endure, I hoped Mrs. Stead wasn't mad at me for not coming back earlier, when I'd said I would. But what I really worried about was my dad not telling it right—about Joey's rampage at Dr. Meiners', and everything else. I knew that getting people to believe you depended on how you told your story.

I knew, also, because of the white coat flapping around his legs, that the man walking briskly at my father's side when he came back to the parking lot was my mother's doctor. We could take Joey in! Otherwise the doctor wouldn't have come outside. He'd have said no to my dad in the building.

I jumped out of the car and ran around to the other side to let Joey out.

"Gary, wait!" called my father, although he was almost to the car. "Don't let him out."

My excitement turned to anger as I decided that this stupid jerk doctor had come to explain to me about germs.

"This is Dr. Hillberry, Gary," said my father. But the doctor was already leaning down over me, with an arm around my shoulder, talking fast into my face. He said he was letting Joey come inside the hospital. He said my mother was hurt very bad, which was why Joey could come in. I could come in, too, but I could not see my mother. I would stand just outside the room she was in. If I wanted to, I could call to her that I was there and that I loved her. That was all. No going close, no seeing her.

"Do you agree to that, Gary?" Dr. Hillberry asked. "Do we have a deal?"

I nodded my head.

He took his arm from my shoulder and straightened. "That's not good enough. Tell me we have a deal and we'll shake on it."

"We have a deal," I said, and I put my hand out first.

After the handshake, Dr. Hillberry turned to my father, and in a gentler tone than he'd used with me, said, "I hope you know that I'm putting my ass on the line."

CHAPTER 7

Limits To Everything

I don't remember walking from the hospital parking lot to the building. After I was standing beside our car and hearing Dr. Hillberry say the forbidden A-word, memory places me inside the hospital, in a wide doorway from which I peered into the room where my mother was.

My father stood behind me with his hands pressed against my chest. I couldn't see my mother, not even the bed she was on. At first I looked mostly at Dr. Hillberry, a tall man who seemed constantly in motion. He was a few feet in front of me, gripping Joey's lead. When he moved over and no longer obstructed my view of the large room, I saw only things . . . machinery, tubing. There was metal and light. There were sounds, too, but a larger silence consumed them.

I made no sound, although I wanted to shout to Joey to hurry. Why wasn't he straining at the end of his lead? Why wasn't he pulling so hard with desire to get to my mother that he dragged Dr. Hillberry off his feet?

It was Joey being dragged by the doctor, not the other way around. I wanted to go in there and take over, but my father's hands restrained me. So did the deal I'd made with Dr. Hillberry, and my fear.

Joey wouldn't be dragged any further. He flattened himself to the floor. Shocked, desperate, trembling against my father, I found the courage to shout, "Joey! Go to Mom!"

He didn't budge. I'd seen the doctor tug on the lead. Now he turned toward me.

"Make him do it!" I shouted.

"I can't. He won't go near her. You've tried with Joey, Gary. Now tell your mother what you want her to know. Talk loud. Shout if you want. She's unconscious but she'll hear you."

He wanted me to shout to my mother when I couldn't even see her. He wanted me not to care if Joey cured her or not. "Joey do it!" I yelled. "Lick Mom and make her well!"

He lifted his head and shoulders and I thought he was getting up to obey. But he started turning in my direction, twisting his head and the front part of his body as if to look over his shoulder at me, and he did it in a slow, stiff motion that seemed unnatural. Then he opened his mouth so wide it made him look scary. He fell, with his neck still twisted, and rolled to his side. His head slapped the floor. His legs stiffened and jerked.

"What the . . . I don't need this!" snapped the doctor.

"He's epileptic," my father said. "My wife just found out yesterday and told me last night before the accident."

I heard in those matter-of-fact words that my father was terribly, terribly beaten. When he relaxed his grip on me, I broke free and ran. I ran out of the hospital to the parking lot. I got inside our car and closed the door. The car was stifling from being in the sun, but I didn't bother to roll the window down. I stared at the dashboard until my father came with Joey.

When they were in the car, I didn't look at either of them. My dad rolled his window down and leaned across me to do mine. He said, "Joey wouldn't go to Mommy because a seizure was coming on. He knew something was wrong with him, and he didn't want to hurt her."

That explanation gave me enough hope to turn and face him and ask, "Did he lick her when the seizure was over."

My father looked at me without speaking. I felt he was deciding whether to tell the truth. "No, he didn't," he finally said. "He just wanted to get outside. He pulled hard and seemed to know his way out. But he was shaky—unsteady on his feet. He had to urinate. Then he wanted to get to the car. To you. He wanted you."

"I don't want him," I said and turned away, staring hard out the window at my side. I knew that Joey hadn't wanted to get to me. He already realized he couldn't be my dog anymore. He hadn't licked or even sniffed me over the car seat.

"Gary—"

"I don't want him!"

"He's just a dog." My father's voice became a little sharp. "I tried telling you that before we came here. He's just a dog and he can't make Mommy well. But he loves us. He loves us very much, and he's—"

I put my hands over my ears but still I heard my father say that Joey was a good dog.

That, and no more. He started the car and we drove home in silence. I thought that I would take Joey to the pound. If my mother died, he would have killed her. If she didn't die but had to be in a wheelchair or was blind the rest of her life, he'd be responsible for that. I could not love him. I was changed. We all were.

Mr. Mooney was standing by the driveway of our house when we drove up. He spoke to my father through the window. Dr. Hillberry had called and my father was to call him.

I left it to my father to let Joey out of the car. Brushing past Mr. Mooney, I went inside to my room and closed the door. When my father knocked a few minutes later, I was standing looking at the vacated dove nest in the tree outside my window. As I turned and crossed the room, I reminded myself that I'd made a vow never to cry, and I must keep it.

I opened the door. My father's face looked contorted. He stopped and slipped his arms around me and in a strangled voice said, "Mommy's gone."

Harsh sobs broke from him. He held me tighter. I squinched my eyes closed and gritted my teeth against his middle.

"I love you," my father whispered. "I'll take care of you."

More sobs came, and they pierced me. I trembled all over. When he spoke again his voice was loud, almost fierce. "Don't be afraid. We'll be okay. We'll take care of each other. We'll get through this. We're strong. We'll get through it. You mustn't be afraid."

But I was afraid, and angry. Why'd she have to die? Didn't millions of people get in car accidents and not die? She could have gotten well without Joey's help. That's why she'd been in the hospital—to get well! She wouldn't do it, though, and now Dad had to cry and I was scared and we had to take care of each other and get through this.

Was it all because I'd treated Chappie nicer than her? I wondered this while gripped in my father's embrace.

The afternoon gave itself over to telephone calls, people coming to our house, and tears in the eyes of everyone but me. My dad called relatives. He made what I kept hearing people refer to as "arrangements." After those few moments in my bedroom, he didn't cry much at any one time but cried all day. His tears seemed like tiny shards slowly falling away from something made of glass, something broken.

People came in and out of the house. My mother's closest friend was one. She put her arms around me and said, "I loved her more than anything, Gary baby. She was the dearest, sweetest friend I'll ever have."

My mother, an only child, had called this woman her sister. I don't remember my mother ever complaining about being lonely in her girlhood, but she'd been only eleven when her father died in an accident while serving in the Army. When she was pregnant with me, her mother, my grandmother, became ill and died.

Of course, I wasn't thinking of my mother's losses while standing rigid and dry-eyed in her friend's arms. I was thinking that my mother could have prevented all this grief. So could Joey, with one lick of his tongue.

Chappie came over and was there when Joey made his one attempt to win my forgiveness. He had not been following me around the house as he usually did. His absence from whichever room I was in had, in fact, made me decide that he was purposely avoiding me. But when Chappie and I sat opposite each other in the breakfast room, where I picked at the belated hot lunch Mrs. Mooney had prepared for me, Joey came and sat beside me and rested his snout on my lap.

"Off," I snarled, pushing him away. He sat still, as if deciding whether or not to try again. I stuck my foot out from under the table and kicked him.

It was a light kick. He didn't flinch or make a sound when I did it. But afterwards he stood and walked away into the kitchen. Chappie rose and followed. Well, if she wanted to comfort him that was fine with me. She could also be the one to see that he had fresh water in his bowl, and give him his dinner tonight and his medicine. I wouldn't do it.

When I took my plate and glass into the kitchen, Chappie was on the floor next to Joey, who was under my mother's desk. Since Chappie still liked him, I decided that maybe I would give him to her instead of taking him to the pound. But I wasn't sure yet, so I didn't say anything, and I didn't stay in the kitchen.

I wanted to be alone and lie down, but not in my bedroom and certainly not in my parents' room. I went to my father's study. It had a small sofa where I could curl up. I was about to close the door when the phone on my father's desk rang. On the first ring I tore over to it and grabbed it and threw it as hard as I could at the bookcase behind the desk.

"Gary," said a voice behind me.

I turned. Mr. Mooney stood in the doorway.

"Put the phone back on the desk, son," he said gently.

As I did that, he closed the door and sat down on the sofa. "Come and sit with me," he said, patting the sofa cushion. "I want to tell you something about your mother."

I sat. I didn't look at him. My eyes blinked a lot.

"Your mother's in heaven, with God, and she's happy there. She is, because it's a better place. But you must remember that she struggled valiantly to live. She wanted to stay here with you and your father. She knew how much you loved and needed her. And she loved you as much as any human being can love another. She would have much preferred to remain here."

He spoke more, but the words slid past me. My mother had struggled valiantly! *Valiantly!*

The word thrilled me. Of course she'd struggled valiantly! She never would have died on purpose. She loved us and knew how much we loved her.

I'd had two stones of resentment pressing on my heart. Mr. Mooney had lifted one away.

Finally, at about nine, the last visitors left. "You'd better go to bed," my father said. Several women had brought food over, and he was filling the dishwasher with plates and glasses.

By the time I was washed and ready for bed, he was sitting in the living room in his usual chair. I said goodnight to him. He was not reading or watching television, and he had not lit a fire in the fireplace, which ordinarily he did on winter nights. I went to my bedroom feeling that his sitting all alone with no warming fire was the saddest thing to have happened yet.

For the first time in my life, I closed my bedroom door when I went to sleep. It was to keep Joey out. But in bed I worried that my father would think I'd closed the door against him. I considered getting up to open it, but decided against. I also decided not to pray.

For a long time I hadn't been saying bedtime prayers aloud with my mother listening, but in silence with only God listening, and not infrequently I'd wondered if God actually did. On this night of my mother's death, I again wondered if God heard prayers, and, if he did, did he care? Thanks to a couple of older boys on our block, I'd become aware of three possibilities regarding God: he existed and listened, he existed but was indifferent, he didn't exist.

My Catholic friend John Mullen was going to be a monk when he grew up. His description of the life of a monk intrigued me, and I thought I might be one, too. Howard Steinberg, on the other hand, had become an atheist. He said God couldn't exist, because if he did there wouldn't be war or poverty anywhere in the world. (Howard's twin sister had become very religious and wore Jewish jewelry and sent Jewish greeting cards to poor Jews in Russia.)

I'd thought of becoming an atheist like Howard, but I'd known my mother would be furious and my dad probably wouldn't like it either. But lying in bed on the night my mother died, I knew that bedtime prayers were over for good, and I would not be a monk.

A few minutes after I'd gotten into bed, my father knocked on the door and then came in. While feeling glad that he wasn't alone in the living room anymore, I hoped he wouldn't ask me to say a prayer.

He sat on the edge of my bed. "Mommy knew how much you loved her," he said softly, brushing the back of his hand across my cheek. "She knew how much you wanted to help her."

"How?" I asked. "She was unconscious and I didn't say anything to her."

"You didn't have to, champ. She knew."

If he was right, then my mother had also known that Joey didn't want to help her. I didn't share this thought with my dad because it would make him feel worse than he already did.

"Gary, I want to discuss with you what you believe about Joey. I know your belief is very strong, but it's unfounded. It goes against everything we know scientifically." I opened my mouth but he didn't let me speak. "Wait, let me finish. It's not only impossible for Joey to have the kind of power you attribute to him, but thinking he has it is unfair to him. To say he could have made Mommy well is to say that he's some kind of god. That isn't so. You know it isn't so."

"Then why did you take him to the hospital?"

"Because I had to. I didn't want to. But I knew I was going to lose Mommy, and if I didn't do what you wanted I would lose you, too. You would have thought I'd robbed her of her chance—"

His voice broke. The bed trembled with his sobs. But in a moment he stopped crying and said, "You would have thought I'd taken your mother from you. You wouldn't have been able to forgive me for that."

I didn't know how to answer, so I said nothing.

"Would you come and sleep with me?" he asked.

The request surprised me so much that I didn't respond.

"Don't if you don't want to," he said. "I'll understand."

"I want to." I sat up. He got up from the bed, and I did, too. When I followed him from the bedroom I left the door open.

I slept on my mother's side of the bed and could smell her cologne on the pillow. My back was pressed against my father's body. He had one arm around my chest and the other curved over my head. "Honey, I don't want you to lose Joey," my father said softly. "You need him. He couldn't help Mommy but he can help you. Trust me Gary that he's a good dog. He would have done anything in the world to help your mother. He would have laid down his life for her."

Honey! He'd never called me that or anything like that. I squinched my eyes closed just in case there were tears in them of which I wasn't aware—and that would try to get out.

He fell asleep; I knew from the rhythm of his body. I began to think about Joey. Where was he? How did he feel? Perhaps in his unhappiness he'd run away. He could have gone out the doggy door and jumped over the fence and disappeared into the night.

I knew two boys in my school whose dogs had run away. One of the dogs, a collie, had been hit by three cars before dying. Joey probably had run away, I decided, but I didn't care. Let him be hit by a car. Let him be picked up and taken to the pound. My mother had struggled valiantly but he wouldn't help her.

Although eventually I fell asleep, that night remains the longest and loneliest of my life. The bedroom door was open but Joey, as far as I know, never came in. Joey always roamed at night. He would sleep beside my bed but never straight through until morning, because he had to check on things. I'd been told by my mother, often, that he paid a nightly visit or two to her and my dad, to check on them. But that night he didn't come to their room.

When I woke in the morning, I was alone. I got up and went to my bedroom to see if Joey had slept there. He'd spent the night in our room, all right, and left a mess of hair on his blanket for evidence. Looking at that blanket, I made a final decision to give Joey to Chappie.

I knew that my dad would try to talk me out of giving away my dog. He'd think it was a big mistake. But whatever he said, I was determined. Chappie would probably think my giving Joey to her was temporary, that I'd get over being angry with him and would want him back. Like hell. That was what Howard Steinberg said a lot. Like hell. I would not take Joey back for anything. And if Chappie thought that I would, and had the nerve to tell me so, I'd hate her for it.

I'd awakened late that Sunday. When I went in the kitchen, my father was on the phone. He mostly listened, saying little. I thought this must be more about "arrangements." Or else he was talking to my Aunt Ellen in South Dakota.

When he hung up he told me that Chappie had been by and would come back later. "I asked her if you'd told her what happened at the hospital yesterday. She said you hadn't, so I did. Do you mind?"

"No," I said. He'd spoken softly, in a tired voice. I wanted to change the subject. "Was that Aunt Ellen on the phone?"

"Dr. Meiners," he answered. "I was lucky to get through to him on a Sunday. He's putting Joey on a higher dosage of phenobarbital because of the seizure he had yesterday. I gave him two pills with his breakfast, while you were sleeping. Now I'll give him another one. He's outside. Want to call him in for me?"

I couldn't say no, but I couldn't do what he'd asked me to do, either.

My father waited a moment and then went to open the door and call Joey inside. I left the kitchen before Joey came in. A while later, after I'd bathed and dressed and had a breakfast of juice and cereal, I went to get Joey myself.

He was on the rear patio, looking dejected in the sunshine. Being careful not to touch him, I attached his leash to his collar. He didn't look at me or touch me either.

Silently, I walked him next door, where we found Chappie working in the backyard. Her deal with the Mooneys was room and board in exchange for doing all the yard work and helping clean house and run errands when her handyperson schedule permitted.

She was on her knees pulling weeds from a flower bed when I brought Joey over. "Hi," I said.

She gave the lift of her chin that meant, "Hi."

"I'm giving Joey away. Do you want him?"

"Why don't you want him?" she asked with her eyes. I answered, "You know why."

She nodded, looking very thoughtful. Then she unclipped her notepad.

"Joey knows his limits and he knew he couldn't help your mother. That's why he wouldn't lick her. It's probably why he had the seizure. Can you imagine his frustration at not being able to heal the injuries of someone he loved more than his own life? Think how you'd have felt in his place. I know how I'd have felt. But if you still think you don't want him, I'll take him. He's the best dog in the world, and would be if he didn't have any power at all except to make people happy."

As I read those words, the other stone lifted. Crisp morning air filled my lungs as if it were the first real breath I'd drawn in a whole day. Everything she'd written was right! I could love Joey again! Of course there were limits to his magic powers! There had to be! Hadn't my father said just a week ago that no one in the world would ever play better tennis than the Australian Rod Laver because there were limits to everything?

I hadn't let go of Joey's lead, but now I did, and I just fell all over him, hugging him and roughing up his fur and kissing his snout. He, in turn, gave me such ferocious nibble kisses that they almost hurt. We kept at this a long while. When we stopped, we were both panting, and he wore that cocky, tongue-lolling grin that I loved so much. His gleaming eyes said, "*I knew all along I was innocent. Isn't it great that you love me again?*"

But of course I hadn't stopped loving him, not for a minute. I'd only turned my love into hate and used it to hurt him, as I'd sometimes done to my mother—only never as cruelly. Joey must have felt so miserable in the hospital, knowing he couldn't help Mom and she was going to die. His heart had been breaking. That's why he'd lain on the floor. Then he'd had the seizure. And I'd rejected him. I'd pushed him away, and kicked him. He'd done nothing wrong, and I'd kicked him.

"I love you," I told him silently, looking deep into his wonderful brown eyes. "I'm sorry I kicked you."

His mouth closed. He puffed.

This funny thing Joey did with his upper lip had always made my parents and me happy. He only did it when he was sitting close to one of us and looking into our eyes, and it didn't happen often enough, not more than a couple of times a week, and usually less. My mother had named it "puffing." My father, when Joey puffed, would say, "Look, Gary. Joey's got snuff in his lip again."

I'd never been able to figure out how or why he puffed out his upper lip, or why he sometimes did it on one side of his mouth only, and other times on both sides—what my dad had named "a full puff."

This time, it was a full puff. If my mother had seen it, she would have asked, "Are you my big puff doggy, Joey?" She would have answered herself, "Yes, you are. You're my big, *big* puff doggy."

In my mind, I saw her smiling at Joey and heard her saying those words. Leaning forward on my knees, I kissed Joey's upper lip on one side and then the other. When I leaned back, he'd stopped puffing, which was what I'd wanted.

Joey and I were to stay at the Mooneys' for several days, to make room at our house for my South Dakota relatives, and so that my cousin Karen, who was allergic to dogs, would not have an allergic reaction to Joey. Karen would have my room, so of course all my bedding was changed, even the spread. While my dad was vacuuming every inch of the house, Chappie came over and took down my curtains and washed them, too.

The relatives were due to arrive Monday, but because of Karen's allergies Joey and I moved next door on Sunday. I was to sleep on the daybed in Mr. Mooney's study, with Joey on his blanket on the floor next to me. Packing my suitcase, going next door with it, being fussed over by Mrs. Mooney, and going back and forth between the two houses all day and evening comprised a huge distraction from numbing tragedy. But when I hadn't seen my father for even a little while, I would feel such a tug of sorrow for him that it was painful. I fantasized at one such moment that when the two of us went to the airport to meet the South Dakota relatives' plane, we would instead get on a plane ourselves and fly to a far-away island where we would live without memories of anything sad. I realized that I would miss Joey and Chappie on the island, so I reinvented the fantasy to include them.

Before he unpacked his suitcase, Uncle Ray told me it was all right to cry. Later, he made me go outside in front with him so he could talk to me privately. "Man to man," he called it. This was Monday evening, after dinner. Only a few stars flecked the sky. Our street was quiet but I could hear cars go by on the boulevard that separated Belmont Shore, where we lived, from Belmont Heights, where people lived in houses that were large and grand.

A big man, Uncle Ray had a face that only knew to smile or frown. Smiling, he gazed upward at the stars and pronounced them unimpressive. "You should see the stars in the Black Hills of South Dakota," he said. "That is a sight."

Abruptly, he lost interest in stars. He put an arm around my shoulders and said, "Gary, I was the kind of guy who wouldn't cry no matter what happened. But when your cousin Alan died, I cried buckets. And boy, I tell you, it was a big help. I'm not saying it took away the hurt, not any of it. But it helped. And it changed me a lot, and for the better. I knew I was more of a man, to be able to cry for someone I'd loved so much."

I wanted to escape from his arm around my shoulders, but didn't dare. I felt like yelling, "Am I supposed to burst out bawling just because you want me to?" My lips could have been glued shut they were so tight.

"Do you understand what I'm saying?" he asked, which meant that I might be too dumb to understand. He pulled me closer to his side, and with his free hand roughed up my hair.

"Yeah," I replied.

"Good. That's my guy. That's my favorite nephew for all time." He'd taken his arm from my shoulders, but I waited until he'd stopped talking before putting distance between us.

"I'm cold," I called over my shoulder as I ran for the house. Inside, I went in the bathroom and stayed there a long time, thinking of the things I should have told my uncle. "You don't get to decide if someone cries or not!" I should have said. "Crying didn't make you more of a man, but you're sure right that it changed you! My dad told us that when he came home after Alan's funeral!"

I didn't like my cousin Karen, who was eleven and starting to get breasts, any better than I liked her father. She said that sleeping in my room made her eyes and nose run, and her throat feel scratchy. But I never saw her use a tissue, and I thought she was just saying it, making a big deal out of nothing.

"How come you never cry for your mom?" she asked on Tuesday morning. She and I were standing in front of my house waiting to go to the funeral. "When my brother died I cried, and so did all his friends. They were boys your age and older. They weren't ashamed to cry. Neither was my dad. Are you scared people will think you're a fairy if you cry?"

Without so much as shrugging, I turned away and pretended to study the trunk of a palm tree in the middle of our front lawn. Karen was a speck of dust. She was yesterday's snot, as the boy who was the troublemaker in my class liked to say. I made a vow to myself that never again would fat-butt Karen Rawls matter in my life. Then I turned and faced her with my eyes and mouth stretched terribly wide like Joey when he had a seizure.

The service for my mother was at the Mooneys' church. I'd never been there before. We sat in front. My mother's casket had white flowers on top of it and was closed. I sat between my father and my Uncle Ray, and felt unhappy that it wasn't Chappie next to me, or Aunt Ellen, or anyone else but Uncle Ray or Karen.

Aunt Ellen was on the other side of my dad, and they held hands throughout the service. People cried and cried. It seemed that sounds of crying came now and again from everyone present except the minister, Chappie, and me. Uncle Ray put his arm around my shoulders. I felt the weight of it even after he took it away. Several times he looked at me in a way that made me feel he was checking for tears.

I didn't have any tears. It struck me that my mother might know I wasn't crying, and I felt terrible about that. She probably did know. Yes, she did. I was certain of it.

For a moment I imagined her listening through the walls of her casket. That was such a gruesome thought that I had to put it out of my mind fast. But some other way, she knew.

Did she think I hadn't loved her and didn't miss her? I fervently hoped not. But I couldn't prove my love for her by crying. I couldn't do that for her. I just couldn't.

CHAPTER 8

Simple Trust

The party at our house began when we returned from the cemetery and lasted into the night. Throughout it I heard much animated conversation that had nothing to do with my mother's dying, and this bothered me. My indignation peaked when I overheard Uncle Ray brag to a teacher from my father's school about the great hunting and fishing in the Black Hills of South Dakota.

"Black Hills of South Dakota," my uncle said over and over that bitter week, never naming Keystone, where he lived. I knew the string of words was meant to impress people.

I interrupted a conversation between my father and Mr. Steinberg in the kitchen to announce that I was going next door.

"No one's there so you'd better not," said my father.

"I want to see Joey," I said. "There's nothing to do here."

"Go find your cousin Karen and ask her to play Monopoly with you in your bedroom."

What an insult! How could he think I would play games that day? I left the kitchen and ambled around the house but found no one I wanted to talk to. I wished Chappie were here. She was in San Pedro, at the home of her friend who would soon have a baby. She'd gone straight from the cemetery to take care of her friend and the friend's little girl, who had the flu. She wouldn't return until after her friend's new baby was born sometime during the week.

When Chappie had explained this plan to me, before we all went to church, my response had been, "Let's take Joey over there to lick the little girl. She'll get well and you won't have to stay."

Chappie wrinkled her nose, which was her way of saying that something wouldn't work. I said, "Why not? Curing the flu's not beyond Joey's limits. Flu's easy for him."

She answered with a note. "I'd have to stay at Nan's anyway. She really needs me. Her husband is worthless around the house. He tries to help but messes up and makes more work. I'm sorry, but I have to be there."

I felt slighted then, and I still did. My need of Chappie was greater than her friend's. Did being pregnant and having a sick kid compare to having your mom die and your home invaded by Karen Rawls? Of course it didn't.

I put on a jacket and went out through the kitchen to the backyard, now in darkness. On the other side of the redwood fence that separated our yard from the Mooneys', Joey whined loudly to attract my attention. Had it been a stranger and not me, he'd have barked.

The fence gapped between two boards. Through that opening, years ago, my friend Bill and I would pass small objects to each other. Shortly after Chappie came to live next door, she folded a note into a tiny square and delivered it to me through the fence, which made that note seem secretive and extremely important. It was the first one I kept. Now my notes from Chappie filled two shoeboxes, a round cookie tin my mother gave me, and half a cigar box given me by Mr. Mooney. Normally, these were on a shelf in my closet, but I'd taken them to the Mooneys' to keep them from Karen's prying eyes.

Joey knew about the fence gap, of course, and I knew he was waiting for me there. After stepping carefully into my mother's narrow border of flowers, I knelt by the fence and poked my fingers through to the other side, where they found Joey's cool, moist nose. He gave a soft moan of pleasure, then licked me.

"I'm sorry I kicked you," I said. "It's the worst thing I've ever done. I'd give anything to take it back."

He barked, but I knew he wasn't answering me. Someone had come outside. I didn't turn around. It could be Uncle Ray or Karen.

"I saw you through the kitchen window," said my Aunt Ellen when she reached the edge of the garden. "How about some company?"

I stood. "Okay." Meager light thrown by the lamp over the kitchen door let me see her nice features. She looked like my dad, only different.

"Did you come outside to talk to your dog?"

"Yeah." I stepped cautiously over violas and onto the lawn.

"How's he getting along? Does he mind staying over there?"

"I guess not."

"Good. I'm glad. The Mooneys are awfully nice. I understand you have a friend who lives with them. Happy? Is that her name?"

"Chappie."

"Chappie. Oh, of course. I've heard she's a very special friend of yours. Do you do lots of things together?"

"I guess."

"I used to have long, long talks with your mother on the phone, Gary. She told me so many things about you. She was always so proud of you. You knew she was, didn't you?"

"Yeah. I guess."

"We ran up horrendous phone bills, your mother and I, but it was worth it. She could always cheer me up when I needed it. She had a happy outlook on life that was contagious."

I said nothing.

"Gary, is it hard having to talk about your mother?"

"I guess."

"I'm sorry, honey." She touched my hair just the way my mom had done a million times. "I thought talking about her might help. But we never really do know what will help another person. We just have to make a guess, and hope we guessed right. Anyhow, tell me about Chappie. What's she like? Is she pretty? Does she go to school?"

I shrugged, pretending not to have answers to these questions. I'd never forgotten my mother saying that Chappie didn't do anything to make herself prettier, and that she could have done better for herself if she'd stayed in school.

"I'd love to meet her," Aunt Ellen said. "I'm sure your Uncle Ray and Cousin Karen would, too."

This loosened my tongue and I quickly said, "You can't. She's helping her friend who's having a baby two weeks early. Her friend's little girl is very sick and her husband is worthless. Chappie has to be there every minute."

"What a wonderful thing for her to do," said my aunt. "But maybe she'll come home while we're still here."

"Did Uncle Ray change after Alan died?" My question came unbidden and startled me.

Aunt Ellen, too, seemed startled. After a moment, her face relaxed and she softly said, "Yes, he did, and I did too. It was just so—oh, Gary. How can I tell you?"

I wanted to say she didn't have to tell me, but I couldn't open my mouth to do it. I'd had no right asking the question. That I'd done it to get her to stop talking about wanting to meet Chappie made me feel even worse.

"We had a son," said my aunt slowly, "and then we didn't. So we became lonely. We hadn't been lonely before. What made it even harder for us was that neither could know what the other had lost. Having a son . . . having Alan, had meant one thing for me, and another for your uncle."

That was *exactly* how it was for me and my dad! He didn't know what I'd lost, and how could I understand what had been taken from him? We were lonely now, and even though we loved each other, and Joey, we couldn't change back to being not lonely.

"Did that help any?" Aunt Ellen asked.

"I guess," I said.

She smiled. "Am I your favorite aunt? Wait. Try not to answer with 'I guess.'"

I almost answered "Yeah" but caught myself in time and smartly said, "Yes, you are. You're my favorite aunt."

"Good. But since I'm the only one you have, the competition isn't too stiff. Come on. Let's go inside."

I liked her tremendously and felt like telling her that if I had six more aunts, she would still be my favorite. But I didn't.

One reason I didn't want my South Dakota relatives to meet Chappie was that afterwards they would talk about her. The other and more profound reason was that I knew my closeness to Chappie had hurt my mother. It wasn't something I'd thought about often during the three years Chappie had lived next door, but sometimes I'd thought about it, most recently at Thanksgiving.

I'd made Chappie a card at school and given it to her the day before the holiday, after showing it to my mother. Above a drawing of a horn of plenty, I'd written, "At Thanksgiving I am thankful for my country, my friend Chappie, and my dog Joey."

My classmates had made similar cards but theirs mentioned parents, and siblings if they had any.

I hadn't thought about what I was doing before choosing Chappie over my parents, but having made the decision I'd known it would be hurtful. I showed the card to my mother but not my father. I felt ashamed watching her look at it.

My mother studied the card with an admiring smile on her lips, then proclaimed, "This is beautiful. Chappie will love it."

"Mine was the best because the fruit looks so real," I boasted. "Everyone said so. The horn is called a cornucopia. Making the fruit look real was really hard. Look at the coconut. That was the hardest because you have to make it look hairy."

"You did a *wonderful* job. The fruit looks real enough to eat. Mmm–I can almost taste the coconut."

My mother's eyes had glowed with pride. "You're a natural-born artist, and an even better friend," she said. "This is going to make Chappie very happy."

She'd sounded sincere. I knew she was sincere. The next day—our last Thanksgiving together—I tried not to think about that card, which Chappie, at Mrs. Mooney's urging, had placed on the hearth mantle in the Mooneys' living room.

Today I ask myself how I'd like it if one of my children preferred the company of a man who lived next door, than mine. I wouldn't like it. I'd hate it. I might even be suspicious of it.

Chappie and my mother had been close in age, but Chappie had been the more youthful, the more athletic, and to me the more interesting. Also, she could converse with me without showing disappointment or approval. Of course the real edge she'd held over my mom was that she hadn't been my mother, or anyone else's.

My mother never said anything resentful about the friendship. I'm certain she didn't worry about seduction. If she intuited that on my part it wasn't a platonic relationship, that I had an enduring crush on Chappie, she never alluded to it.

My father went back to school. His goal, to earn a Ph.D. in geophysics and then work for a major corporation, would take five years to achieve. While commuting to Los Angeles for night classes, and researching and writing his doctoral thesis, he continued in his career as a high-school teacher and assistant tennis coach. During those years I saw a lot less of him than I had in the past, and more of Chappie and Mr. And Mrs. Mooney. It was as if the pink stucco house next door, from which I'd once been cruelly evicted, had become my second home. It was also a second home for Joey. We entered it together whenever we wanted, without knocking—always sure of feeling welcome.

I was ten when Chappie and Joey and I took a walk in Recreation Park on a sunny April day and Joey terrified an old man out of ten years of his life.

Joey had been walking a few feet ahead. As I related to Chappie a story that my teacher, Mr. Bell, had told the class, about when he was a fighter pilot in Vietnam, I let the lead dangle loosely from my fingers.

Suddenly Joey broke away from me and ran up to three old men and an old woman sitting at a picnic table.

"Get away! Get off me! Somebody help!" yelled one of the men.

Chappie and I reached the scene at the same time. Joey's forepaws were on the lap of the man, who, sitting facing away from the table, apparently was trying to keep Joey from licking his chest.

I felt certain that Joey was saving this stranger from dying of a heart attack, so certain that I stopped breathing and didn't move.

Chappie grabbed Joey by the collar and pulled him back, then scooped up the end of his lead. The man's hands, half clenched into fists, trembled against his chest. They were the ugliest hands I'd ever seen, and they glistened with Joey's saliva.

"I just lost ten years of my life! Are you crazy? You can't let a dog run wild in a park! It's against the law! What's the matter with you? You're brainless, that's what! Go on! Get him out of here!"

He'd directed all this at Chappie. Feeling great indignation, I said, "He's my dog. He wanted to help you. He thought you were having a heart attack."

The other two men, with a checkerboard between them, thought this was hilariously funny and laughed and coughed and spat accordingly. The woman pulled a tissue from her sweater pocket and honked her nose.

"If I have a heart attack, I'll sue your parents!" shouted the man Joey had licked. He lowered his hands to wipe them on the shiny brown material that covered his withered thighs. "That dog'll turn against you some night while you're asleep. He'll rip your throat open. You wait!"

He shut up suddenly, although his lips continued to move. He stared at his hands. So did I. He spread his fingers, then flexed them. Slowly, he lifted his hands and held them out in front of his face.

As disbelief widened his eyes, disgust narrowed mine. He hadn't been having a heart attack. He'd had warts on his hands. Barf! Triple barf! I'd wash Joey's mouth with a garden hose ten times before letting him kiss me again.

Another man said, "Hey, the dog did that! He cured your arthritis, Owen."

Owen snapped, "Who says it's cured? It's just a little better."

"A helluva lot better! I'd like my left foot to be that much better."

Turning red-rimmed eyes on Joey, this enthusiastic man said, "Do me, big fella. Cure old B.J.'s foot. I've got a bunion, corns, and heel spurs for you to work on."

He pulled off a sandal and sock, exposing a foot that turned my stomach. I looked at Joey, sitting between Chappie and me. His doleful expression said he wished he were somewhere else. Chappie reached in front of him and handed me the lead as if saying, "He's your dog. You decide."

"Come on, doggy," said B.J. He stuck out his foot and wiggled it.

I had returned my gaze to that awful foot, then looked at Joey again. Anyone seeing his expression would have interpreted it as asking: "Do I have to?" But of course he did, and he knew it.

With ears and tail down, Joey slouched forward, stopping just shy of the brown, broken toenails that led to worse signs of spoilage. I squinched my eyes closed.

When I opened them, it was done. Joey had already returned to my side and had plopped down on the grass. His front paws made frenzied swipes at his muzzle.

B.J. did a sort of dance, turning in a circle. "Hey! I could kick ass with this foot! I could do kung fu with it!"

The one called Owen said to the woman, who again was blowing her nose into a tissue, "Let the mutt cure your cold, Virginia. Put your nose down for him to lick."

I remembered hearing my mother say that only time can cure a cold. Sure enough, Joey refused all urging from the old folks to get to his feet, let alone kiss the lady.

"Hah! The dog thinks your nose is uglier than my foot, Virginia," chortled B.J.

I knew this wasn't so and didn't want the lady to think she was ugly. "He knows his limits," I told her. "He can't do colds."

We continued on our walk. I exulted to Chappie that Joey would become famous and I'd be a millionaire. "He'll cure thousands and thousands of people! Most things people get sick with are within his limits. We already know he can do arthritis and heel spurs. Do you see all the commercials there are on TV for arthritis medicine? *Zillions* of people have arthritis."

Chappie stopped on the path to write a short note. "Zillions of people have hemorrhoids. Do you want Joey to cure those?"

If hemorrhoids were where I thought they were, Chappie had just suggested the most sickening thing I'd heard in my whole life. Folding the note and shoving it down in my jeans pocket, I said, "Of course not. Mostly it'll be stuff like pulled muscles. You know—"

I thought hard and came up with: "tennis elbow! You wouldn't believe how many people get that! My dad tells me all the time. And what about the guys who get beat up playing football?"

She started walking again, but my having to keep pace with her long strides didn't stop my outpour. "Hangovers! He'll just lick the guy's head and the guy won't puke anymore! And how about swimmer's ear? And black eyes? One lick from Joey, and presto your black eye's gone. A lot faster and cheaper than putting raw steak on it!"

But instead of matching my enthusiasm, Chappie looked worried. When we came to an empty bench, she sat down and unclipped her notepad. I stayed standing. She wrote furiously and when finished thrust the note at me. She'd written so fast, it was almost illegible.

"Gary, once the world knows about Joey, he'll be taken away from you. He'll be caged in a lab, probably in Washington, D.C. Scientists will do tests on him to see what makes him tick. They'll even cut into his brain. You'll never see him again. Even if the scientists don't kill him, he'll miss you so much he'll have a seizure cluster and die. You won't be a millionaire and you won't have Joey. Do you want that? If you don't, keep quiet."

Now I needed to sit down, and did, next to Chappie. Everything she'd written was right, as usual.

Joey put his paws up on my lap and licked my chin, my mouth, and my closed eyes. I loved him so much. If he were taken from me, I'd die.

Silently, I promised Joey I would never tell anyone about his magic powers. If people guessed, I'd say there were crazy.

At dinner that night my dad asked, "What's new? How was your day" We were having spaghetti, my favorite of the things he cooked.

"It was okay."

"Do anything special after school?"

I shrugged, shook my head, and for extra effect scrunched up my jaw in the way that means "Nah." What I didn't do was look him in the eye.

"Well, I had an interesting day," my father said. He began telling me about it, but I didn't pay attention. I trusted Chappie more than my own father. I was closer to her. My poor dad. He had no one, really, except me and Joey, yet I couldn't let him in our secret.

"You're not listening, are you? You're a million miles away."

He didn't sound irritated, or hurt; nor did his eyes show displeasure. They showed clarity, undemanding need, perhaps amused remembrance of his having been, long ago, what I was now.

I rose from my side of the booth and went to him and wrapped my arms around him.

He returned the hug so fiercely that he nearly pulled me down on his lap. Embarrassed, I broke away and sat back down.

"The spaghetti's good," I said, then shoveled a forkful into my mouth. For the time it took me to chew and swallow, my dad remained silent. When he spoke, his voice was scratchy in a way I hadn't heard since the day of my mother's funeral.

"Did we ever tell you how we got Joey?"

We. It sounded as if my mother were alive, or hadn't been dead very long. She'd died sixteen months ago. I kept count.

"Uh-uh, you didn't," I said.

He cleared his throat. "Well, we'd gone to the animal shelter intending to choose a small dog that wouldn't get too big. But Mommy saw this German shepherd puppy and right away she wanted it. The fellow who was showing us around said, 'Some really weird foreign guy who was dressed strange and had a long beard brought that one in last week. He said he was going home to his own country and couldn't take a dog with him.'"

"What country was it?" I asked, wondering where Joey would be living now if the man had taken him.

"That I don't know. But according to this fellow at the pound, the man said he woke up one morning and there the puppy was, in his apartment. The door had been locked, and the windows were closed. He said he tried to find the dog's owners but couldn't. So he kept him and named him Jodo Shinshu."

"Jodo Shinshu?" I looked down at Joey, napping by my feet. No way could he be Jodo Shinshu.

"Yep. Jodo Shinshu. The fellow at the pound renamed him Joey, which your mother and I liked a whole lot better. But I looked Jodo Shinshu up in the dictionary when we brought Joey home, and it's a Buddhist sect. Its adherents—that means followers—believe that the path to salvation isn't religious ritual, but simple trust."

Simple trust. I was back to feeling bad about my secret from him.

"What's wrong?" my dad asked.

"Nothing."

"Are you sure? You look a little upset."

"I'm not. I'm just thinking about Joey getting into that apartment when the door was locked and the windows were closed. How'd he do that?"

My father smiled a little. His voice had lost its scratchiness. "It's something to think about," he said.

Joey and I were sprawled on the grass in the Mooneys' backyard on a hot October afternoon when I was still ten. Joey slept, snoring softly. I watched Chappie strip the finish from a small piece of furniture. Her tennis shoes, and the spindly feet of the little table or desk, sank into a white sheet she used to protect the lawn.

Wearing shorts and a white dress shirt that had been discarded by Mr. Mooney, Chappie looked more beautiful than any movie actress I'd seen. Her long legs, tanned and athletic, gleamed in the sun. The only blemish on either of them was a fleck of furniture finish that had fallen to her left knee. Was that where the bruise had been? The one Joey made disappear? Although I couldn't remember, my wondering about it led to something else.

"Do you think Joey could cure your throat or tongue or whatever keeps you from talking?" I asked. Immediately, I wished I hadn't. She might think I'd like her more if she could talk. And it would have been impossible for me to like Chappie more. I loved her and intended to marry her when I grew up. Her muteness didn't bother me. I just thought, sometimes, that she might enjoy being able to talk, and not have to write notes all the time.

"Go inside and get me a soda, will you?" she asked with hand and face gestures.

I went to the house. From the kitchen window, I saw her go over to Joey and squat down next to him. She stroked his head, then his muzzle. Wakened by this attention and no doubt feeling happy, he licked her hand.

Chappie thrust her head forward, submitting her throat to be licked. Joey obliged. Afterward, it seemed to me that Chappie was moving her mouth, only I couldn't be sure. I did see her stick out her tongue for Joey to kiss. He did it, too. I grinned.

Getting the bottle of soda out of the fridge and opening it, I felt sure that Chappie still couldn't talk. I took the drink out to her. She thanked me with her eyes, and smiled.

Joey was right, of course. Silence isn't sickness.

I wasn't a horny little boy. I didn't try to imagine what Chappie looked like naked, and never had sexual fantasies about her. There was a recurrent dream, though, that began when I was seven or eight and continued into my fourteenth year.

It came infrequently and each time was different but the essential components were Chappie, me, the Pacific Ocean, and two luminous, grinning dolphins.

Dressed for swimming, Chappie and I would be sitting with our backs pressed together, most often on wet sand at the water's edge but sometimes on a jetty rock, or the pier, or in a small, moored sailboat. Sometimes Joey was with us, sometimes not. Invariably, it was night and the stars were out.

The dolphins would appear and with eager glances summon us to mount them for a ride. How effortlessly we did that! The most exquisite pleasure to be had from these dreams came from floating down from the pier, or the jetty, to land soft as a cloud astride my dolphin, and then to look at Chappie astride hers.

We rode out to sea, to chains of small islands, and wove all around these specks of moonlit mountain. The dolphins would only skim the phosphorescent ocean waves, and never dip below them.

After one dream I woke feeling bad about Joey. If this wonderful thing with the dolphins really were to happen one night, what about him? Would he wait on the beach for us to come back, and worry that we never would? I hoped that from then on, when I had the dream, he would have a dolphin to ride, too. But he never did.

The last of these dreams—which had no ending, no return to shore or dismounting of the dolphins—happened early in my fourteenth year. I remember it more clearly than the others not because it was the last, but because the next day Chappie told me she was in love.

He was a lawyer. They'd just met. Fresh out of law school, he lived in a rented house only a few blocks from us. She was going to do some repairs for him, on furniture he'd inherited from his grandmother. Did I want to meet him, she asked.

I did not, but when saying so I carefully hid my bitter hurt, and my fury. Hadn't I always been faithful to Chappie? And I didn't have to be. Lots of girls liked me. They thought I was cute. In fact, I could have almost any girl in my grade for a girlfriend, if I wanted. Girls called me on the phone and sent me love notes, both anonymous and signed. Laurel Carpenter, the prettiest girl in my algebra class, had said I looked just like Paul McCartney, and had offered to go steady with me. I'd told her, "Thanks, but some other time." I told all the girls who called me at night that I had to get off and do my homework. I read their love notes and threw them away. Chappie's notes to me now filled four shoeboxes in my closet.

I hid my feelings of hurt and anger over Chappie being in love, just as for years I'd hidden my adoration for her.

The hurt and anger diminished. Days came when I forgot I had a competitor for Chappie's affection. But on the day when she said she loved someone else, those dolphins of my dreams dove deep beneath the ocean waves. They hide there still.

CHAPTER 9

How'd You Like Pie In Your Face?

By all appearances we were rolling in dough. My dad had bought a new car and had given me a ten-speed Schwinn for my fourteenth birthday. The next month, for Christmas, he'd had me choose all new furniture for my bedroom, and also surprised me with a new stereo. We talked about renting a camper in the summer and going to redwood country. Of course the trip depended on whether he could get away from the office. If we went, Joey would go with us.

Joey now had a seizure once a month, like clockwork my father said, trying to make light of an ongoing situation that always frightened me. I feared that the single seizure would mushroom into a lethal cluster. In fact, Joey never did have more than two seizures in one day, and thanks to his medication, that seldom happened.

We gave him Phenobarbital and potassium bromide every day. Even with these powerful sedatives in him, he acted like an ordinary dog. Rising to his feet when he'd been lying down was slow going, though, and when he walked he tended to cross his rear legs in front of each other, just slightly. People sometimes asked his age in a way that told me they thought he was very old. And we were sometimes asked if he had a hip problem, which he didn't.

My father often said that Joey was a tough dog who could take it. There was ample evidence that this was so. The things he'd done as a puppy—chase and fetch, run and jump on the beach—he still did. That other dogs ran faster and jumped higher didn't matter because Joey was the best. And he had magic powers.

I never got sick, never caught what was going around. An occasional bellyache or abrasion occurred but disappeared when Joey licked me. My dad, Chappie, Mr. Mooney, and Mrs. Mooney never became ill, either.

Maybe Mr. Hotshot Lawyer, who had fixed Chappie lunch on the Saturday afternoons she worked for him, would get sick and waste away to a ninety-pound weakling. I'd take Joey to him and we'd make a deal: a cure in exchange for his moving away and never contacting Chappie again. He'd also have to promise not to reveal how he regained his health.

I considered the remote possibility of getting rid of the lawyer in this manner while lying on my bed one night in March. Joey was stretched out on the floor beside me, snoring softly. A more plausible scenario than Joey's saving Mr. Assbite Attorney's life was the jerk's getting drafted and sent overseas. Or, after losing a case in court, he might be shot in the head by his enraged client.

These musings had been prompted by Chappie confiding to me that afternoon that she was going to ask the guy out on a date.

"He's supposed to ask," I quickly reminded her.

"Not since women's lib," she wrote just as quickly.

While I read that, she tore off another piece of paper and wrote, "We're meant for each other. I'm not going to let something as unimportant as who does the asking get in the way of our destinies being fulfilled."

What crap! It was on the tip of my tongue to say, "If you're meant for each other, why hasn't he asked you out yet?" But that would be mean, so I asked instead, "How do you know you're in love when you've just had lunch with him a couple of times?"

"I just know," she wrote. "You do, when it happens. Wait. You'll see."

I'd already seen. I'd loved Chappie from the start. "Maybe he'll think you're too old for him," I said.

She looked thoughtful before writing, "That doesn't matter anymore either. Actually, his being younger is a plus. Women live longer than men. I don't want to be all alone when I'm old."

Chappie really was going to marry this guy, and nothing I could say would stop her. This was my brooding thought when my father came to my room. I didn't have music on, so I'd left the door open, and he came in.

He sank into my swivel desk chair. "Gary, I've got something to tell you," he said. But he just stared at me. Finally, he said, "Oh, boy," then swiveled all the way around twice.

Alarmed, I sat up and asked, "Are you getting married?"

"Who me?" he asked, looking surprised. "Are you?"

"Then what is it?"

"It's . . . . Let me recover from your question first. Geez, I never even go out on a date, and you're trying to marry me off."

Tense from all this stalling, I said, "Tell me."

His look turned serious again. "Gary, my firm's sending me to Japan for a year. I'm supposed to leave next month."

"What about me?" I asked, probably with a dumb look on my face. The thought of going to Japan for a year, and leaving in just one month, both excited and appalled me. I was about to ask another question—whether or not Joey would have to be quarantined when we got to Japan—but he began talking again. "Aunt Ellen and Uncle Ray already know that you're coming to stay with them, and they're thrilled. If it were up to them, it would be two years. Karen's excited too, of course. She'll love having someone around who listens to the right kind of sounds." He moved his shoulders in a way that was meant to be cool.

"I don't want to go." My voice came out a croak.

"Of course not, but you'll have a great time. The year will fly by, and before you know it you'll be home, complaining that you miss skiing, and fishing the creek that's practically in the back yard. Trout fishing is *great* in the Black Hills. And you'll water-ski on the lake, of course. They own a boat, remember? It's a great one."

Great this and great that, when it was all crap. "I won't stay with them a whole year!" I practically shouted, and I was not a teenager who shouted at his father. "It's crazy!"

"No, it's not," he answered firmly. "It's a solution. It's the only way I can pull this thing off."

Angrily, already knowing what the answer would be, I hurled, "What about Joey?"

"He can't go."

Hearing it said made it a gut blow. I felt on the verge of tears, and of putting my fist through the wall. How could my father do this to me—and to Joey? Didn't anything matter to him anymore, except money? I didn't voice the question but accursed him with my eyes.

"I know, Gary. That part's the killer. I feel awful about it. If Karen wasn't allergic to dogs, he would go with you. Since he can't, I was hoping Chappie would take care of him. I've already spoken to Mr. And Mrs. Mooney about it. It's fine with them."

"It's not fine with me! Joey will be nine in a year! That's old age for a German shepherd! I can't miss a whole year of his life! You'll never get me to go to South Dakota! I'll run away with Joey if you try to separate us!"

"Gary, listen to me a moment, will you? Then it'll be your turn to talk."

But I couldn't stop. I cried, "Karen isn't allergic to dogs! That's so phony! She just doesn't like them! If she's allergic, why doesn't she get shots so she won't be anymore? I'm not going there! If Joey gets to stay with the Mooneys, I will too."

He fixed me with a look that said it was time to calm down. I closed my mouth and kept it closed, but my jaw trembled. *Jesus! A whole year! Jesus!*

"Okay," he began. "Here's how it is. This is my chance to become a vice president in the firm. That's been told to me, not in so many words but not in a way that was subtle, either. All right, we know what's in it for me. What's in it for you is a first-rate education, the kind that your mother hoped and prayed you would have. Gary, you've been talking about wanting to be a veterinarian, and that's going to cost a fortune. But I want it for you. And I want to go to Japan. I feel that it's right. But I can't go unless you stay with Aunt Ellen and Uncle Ray. I *won't* go if you can't handle it. And if I don't go—listen to me now—there will be no resentment. I won't hold it against you. You'll never hear me mention it."

He'd said all this slowly. After a pause he said, "Okay. Your turn."

Any kid who's had a shitty situation presented to him rationally, and then been told it's his turn to talk, knows what he's stepping into. The foretaste of defeat made my voice whiny when I asked, "Why can't Joey and I go with you?"

"That wouldn't work. I'll be all over the country, not just in one place."

"Then let me stay at the Mooneys, too."

"Sorry, no. I can't ask them that."

"Why? They'd let me."

"I'm sure they would. But they aren't our relatives, and they're very old. It wouldn't be right."

"It's not right for me to go away from Joey for a whole year!"

After saying that, I couldn't meet my dad's eyes. He didn't care about leaving me for a year, or about making me leave my dog, Chappie, and all my friends at school. And I was a boy whose mother had been dead for five years.

My father leaned forward on the chair to stroke one of Joey's ears. The ear twitched once, then was still. Joey sighed in his sleep. "When you go away to college, you'll leave him again," said my father.

"I'm not going away to college. I don't want to be a veterinarian. I'm not going to be anything you have to go to college for, and for sure I'm not going to be a veterinarian."

"Well, feel free to change your mind. And if you do go away to a university four years from now, Joey's likely to still be around."

To that I made no response. If I verbalized my doubts that Joey would beat the odds on his expected lifespan, fate might take it as an invitation to prove me right.

My dad could always read my silences. "Gary, Joey's a tough dog. The seizures aren't going to kill him, and he can take this separation. It isn't as though he'll be with strangers. The Mooneys are his friends."

"I'll go to Long Beach State if Joey's still alive," I said threateningly.

"That'll be your decision to make."

I'd lost, as I'd known I would. But the pain I felt in my heart begged for relief, and I asked, "Do you think he'll still be alive when I graduate college?"

"He might be. That wouldn't make him the world's oldest German shepherd." He smiled a little. "Maybe the second oldest."

I looked down at Joey, lying on his side. Then I slid from the bed to the floor and lifted his head onto my lap. Softly, I stroked his muzzle. His eyes were mostly closed but open just enough for me to see the color and silken glow of his irises. Some German shepherds' eyes slitted up, wolf-like, when they slept, but Joey wasn't like that. He had the intelligence and wisdom of a wolf, but not the look.

I didn't raise my eyes to meet my father's when I mumbled, "You can go."

He placed a hand on top of my head and kept it there, firm against my scalp, for a long moment. When he took it away he said, "Want to go out and get something to eat?"

"We already ate." A teacher at his school had invited us over. He hadn't seemed to have anything weighing on his mind during dinner at Miss Mangelsen's, or on the ride home.

"Who's stopping us from eating again, then taking a walk on the beach? Joey can come with us."

It was late, a school night, and we'd never done anything like that before. I said, "It's almost time for his pills."

"Give them to him when we get home. It'll just be a little late. I wouldn't do it before we go because he might get too drowsy for a walk."

"Okay." I got up to get Joey's leash.

We shared a hamburger with fries and a piece of apple pie at Hof's, then stopped at Safeway to buy magazines. My father would spring for as many rock magazines as I wanted that night, I believed, but I limited myself to two.

On the beach, walking across a football-field width of sand, leading to the water's edge, my father kept an arm around my shoulders. Neither of us spoke until he said, "We're all talked out, I guess," and then, again, we walked in silence. I felt close to him, and resentful of him. Awed by what was to happen the following month, I didn't fully believe yet that it would happen. Moments of excitement for the adventure, the downhill and water-skiing, the trout fishing, would catch me off guard, and then I would wonder if I'd given in too easily. Had I been wrong not to hold firm, and keep him from going away?

We stopped. I stared out at the ocean, which had played so large a role in my life. Snow didn't interest me. Lakes didn't. Neither did fishing in a creek. Joey sat down in front of me. My hand went to his muzzle. My fingers trailed over the long black whiskers which were at one time firm and pliable. Would he remember me, and forgive?

"Look at the moon," my father said.

I looked up at him. He'd tilted his head way back. "Hurry," he said. "Before it falls."

Falls? I tilted my head back to look. The moon was right above us: heavy, white, slashed in two.

"It looks like half a cream pie turned upside down," said my dad, and he joked, "How'd you like pie in your face?"

For a month I did everything in my power to hide my sadness from Joey. If he knew I was miserable, he would be, too. My greatest fear was that stress would cause him to have more frequent seizures, or even the dreaded cluster.

On a Sunday morning in April, shortly before my dad and I were to leave for the airport in Los Angeles, I took Joey next door to give him over to Chappie's care. Mr. And Mrs. Mooney had already left for church when I let myself, and Joey, in through the front door and went looking for Chappie in the kitchen. I'd said goodbye to the Mooneys the day before.

Slouched on a chair at the table, wearing her customary uniform of shorts and shirt, Chappie looked different than I'd ever seen her. The dissimilarity was in her green eyes, which were dull, red-rimmed, and puffy from crying. Her nose was red, too. That my going away would affect her so much actually embarrassed me. More than that, I felt sabotaged. She knew how hard I'd worked to keep Joey from getting upset.

"Hi," I said. "Well, here he is."

She gave me a doleful look that reminded me of a lame bloodhound I'd seen at Dr. Meiners' once. I quickly glanced away, setting my attention on a blue envelope lying on the cloth covered table. Apparently, Chappie had written me a farewell letter. That, I didn't mind. Putting on paper her feelings about my leaving was appropriate. But gloom and doom in front of Joey wasn't.

Joey had gone right to Chappie to be petted. She ignored him at first, then stroked him listlessly between the ears.

"He'll need a lot of love, especially the first month or so," I informed her with just a tinge of reproach in my tone. "I guess he'll need all the attention you can give him the whole year. But it's got to be happy attention. If you love him and act sad at the same time, he'll worry. Dogs can go wild with worry, Chappie. It can affect their health. They stop eating, just like people who are depressed."

My little lecture had no effect. Chappie kept stroking him half-heartedly. He tired of it and trotted off to the service porch for a drink. For years the Mooneys' had kept a plastic water bowl there for him. He came back with his big red rubber bone in his mouth. When he looked at me with an expression that asked how do you suppose this got in the Mooneys' laundry room, my knees went wobbly. He was so innocent. He didn't suspect a thing.

"I guess my dad didn't forget anything," I said to Chappie, forcing cheer into my voice. Earlier, my father had brought Joey's food, pills, liquid medication, blanket, brush, leash and chew toys over. My bedroom had seemed strange and empty without the orange blanket on the floor, and our kitchen counter had also looked unfamiliar without Joey's medicine on it.

Joey took the toy to Chappie and placed it on her lap. She didn't smile or praise him. When the bone rolled off her lap, she acted as if she didn't notice. Joey looked once at the toy, once at Chappie, and then sank to the floor, giving up on her.

"I'm sad, too, Chappie," I said, my tone a little hot. "But it could be a lot worse. What if my dad and I were moving away, forever, and you wouldn't see me again? At least I'll be back in a year. Try not to take it so hard. Can't you do that for Joey's sake? Come on. We talked about this. You know what's at stake."

I didn't want to mention seizures. I always avoided talking about them in front of Joey.

She gave me a wan smile. Then she leaned forward, circled her arms on the table, and cradled her head there.

I didn't want or need this, and Joey sure as hell didn't, either. She was making my leaving harder. But showing her I was angry wouldn't make things better. I had to cheer her up. "I'll write every day," I promised. She didn't respond. Now what should I do? Maybe I should grab her by the shoulders and shake her, but I didn't have the guts. I considered joking her out of her depression by saying, "Buck up, old chum. It'll be ducky after tea." My P.E. teacher, or I should say my former P.E. teacher as of yesterday, who was from England, said this quite often and the class always cracked up when he did.

But when I saw Chappie's shoulders shake with silent sobs, I decided to reason with her. I said, "I guess right now it's Joey we should be concerned about, not ourselves. I mean, we can deal with my leaving, because we know when I'm coming back. And we can write letters to each other. Joey won't know when I'm coming back, and he can't get letters from me, so he's the one who'll suffer most. Unless we both act happy, like nothing's wrong."

She lifted her head and smiled wanly again—the smile of someone who's going to be beheaded and who's being a good sport about it. Impulsively, I said, "Buck up, old chum. It'll be ducky after tea."

God that sounded stupid! Chappie's smile became a grimace. She unclipped her notepad. Thinking she was going to tell me how dumb I'd sounded, I said, "My P.E. teacher says that all the time. It's sure dumb, isn't it?"

She began writing but interrupted herself to point at the envelope on the table, then at me.

I picked up the blank, unsealed envelope. The letter I pulled from it was from Mr. Mooney. He'd written his name, address, and telephone number at the top. Beneath the date he'd written:

Dear Gary,

When you find yourself wondering how Joey is, call to find out. Mrs. Mooney and I are home quite a lot during the day, as you know, and almost always in the evening. The time in South Dakota will be two hours later than here. Dial O and tell the operator that you wish to make a collect call to anyone, and give her our number.

Gary, all unhappiness grows old and fades. Even when fresh it can be lessened by positive and rational thinking. Remind yourself that Joey is in safe, comfortable surroundings and that God, in making him a dog, spared him the burden of time. Just as Joey will never doubt your eventual return, he won't know how long he's waited or how long he has yet to wait.

Mrs. Mooney and I are honored by your friendship. You are an exceptionally fine young man: generous, brave, honest. You remind us of our sons, Lester and Harry, taken from us by war.

Mr. Mooney had signed off with God bless, followed by his initials. I put the letter back in its envelope, folded it in two and slipped it into my pants pocket knowing I would keep it forever.

Chappie had finished writing her note, which, of course, I would keep no matter what it said. I took it from her and read: "I sort of know what you're feeling. Yesterday I asked the man I'm in love with if he wanted to go out with me. He said no. Now I'll never see him again. It's not the same thing as you not seeing Joey for a year, but it hurts. My heart is broken too."

She'd been crying for him! I'd made a complete ass of myself! She must think me a conceited idiot. My mind raced to think of something to say. Silently, I tried out: *I thought that was the real reason you'd been crying. I pretended to think you were upset because I'm leaving. I knew he wasn't interested in you, but didn't want you to be humiliated by knowing I knew.*

That sounded pretty good. I opened my mouth to say it but was stopped by Chappie's next surprise. Abruptly, she got down on the floor and buried her face in Joey's neck. Now I knew she really was hurting. I felt bad for her, but mostly I was frustrated. How could she cheer Joey up after I left if she couldn't cheer herself up?

"He'll probably change his mind and want to go out with you," I said. "You just shocked him by asking him first. He wanted to be the one to ask first. You'll see. He'll change his mind."

But I didn't believe any of this. By throwing herself at the lawyer, she'd ruined her chance with him forever. Men don't like women making advances at them. This I knew from personal experience.

She kept snuggling Joey. Her fingers were curled around his chin and he licked them. Seeing this, I wondered if he had the power to cure her broken heart. I also wondered how to say goodbye to someone who was lying on the floor and wouldn't look at me.

My quandary was interrupted by the phone ringing. I went to the counter to answer it. "Mooneys' residence," I said crisply into the receiver.

It was my father. He wanted me home. We had to leave.

"I have to go," I told Chappie, feeling wobbly-kneed again. This was it. Goodbye. She would stand and hug me. I'd never been in her arms before. I stared at her long legs, radiantly golden where morning light from a half-curtained window slanted across them. Would our legs touch? Would I feel her breasts?

She didn't get up. She rolled off Joey and stretched out on her side, lying on the speckled linoleum almost nose to nose with him. With one hand she caressed his muzzle. With the other she stroked his side. His eyes were open and he looked very content. Her eyes were closed and she looked sad, but less than before, and sort of peaceful. What about me? Should I get down on my knees and give each of them a kiss on the cheek?

I decided not. That Chappie seemed not to care that I was leaving didn't make me as angry as I might have been, because now she was being loving to Joey. Besides, she had a broken heart. I understood that feeling, and I felt glad that she had Joey to help her get over it. Less generously, I reflected that she couldn't get over it too soon, because she was acting weird enough to be put away in a nut house.

I'd said goodbye to Joey many times in the last twenty-four hours. Kissing him now would hurt too much. But I needed to touch him one last time. Squatting on my heels, I slid my hand down the length of his tail—mostly black on the outside and mostly tan underneath. His tail was the part of him I thought most vulnerable to harm. My father had implanted this worry. He'd warned me when we got Joey that I must always be careful not to close a door on his tail, because once it was broken it couldn't be fixed. Consequently, the German shepherd's tail, which nearly touches the floor when hanging down, is the one thing I consider a mistake in the breed.

I closed my hand around the end of Joey's tail. *Goodbye, Joey. I'll miss you. But I'll come back to you.*

For Chappie I had no words, not even silent ones. She'd be all right. Joey would make her better. At least I didn't have the lawyer to worry about anymore.

Outside the Mooneys' house, on the walled front porch, in bright sunlight, the full wallop of separation hit me. I turned and stared at the closed door, and felt my face crumple as if to cry. Joey couldn't witness my pain now. Nothing I did would hurt him as long as I didn't yell or scream. I was free to let it out.

Tears didn't come. I pressed my hands and gaping mouth against the closed door. It tasted of dust and painted wood. *I don't want to go,* I screamed silently. Then I stepped back from the door, composed my features, turned, and walked home.

CHAPTER 10

Grandma Louise Says Outrageous Things

"What a jerk," said my father when someone nearly forced us off the freeway. His next words were, "Did you know that in South Dakota you're old enough for a learner's permit?"

I hadn't known, didn't care, and didn't answer.

"Not that I approve of kids fourteen driving," he continued amicably, as though we were having a two-way, civil conversation. "But South Dakota isn't asking my opinion. Uncle Ray told me he's willing to teach you to drive if it's okay with me." He glanced over at me. "What do you think? Should it be okay?"

I maintained my silence, fuming inside because he was pretending everything was fine.

"Don't care about driving right now?" he asked.

I sighed wearily to show that I couldn't be bothered to even think about it.

"Gary, are you frightened?"

"*Hell,* no," I sneered. "I just don't know if I want Uncle Ray teaching me anything." I studied my lap, fearing a bawling out that might last until we reached the airport.

"I'm not talking about driving now," said my father, showing no irritation. "Are you frightened about going away?"

"No." I turned and stared out the side window. The morning had become hot. The shrubs bordering the freeway were coated with dust. Faintly brown sky belted the horizon.

"Gary, we can turn around and go home. I told you I wouldn't go to Japan if you couldn't handle it."

I faced forward again and said in a tone both churlish and resigned, "I can handle it. I just don't like it."

"I don't like it either. I don't like you having to leave Joey behind. I don't like it one bit. But I expect the year in South Dakota to be a fantastic experience for you. I also have good feelings about Joey staying with the Mooneys. He's going to be a shot in the arm for them. They'll benefit enormously from his company."

An image of Mr. and Mrs. Mooney, and Chappie, with Joey in their living room made me so sad with loneliness that I forgot to sound angry when I said, "Chappie will benefit too."

"I'm sure of it," agreed my father. After we rode in silence a minute or so, he said, "Since yesterday I've been kicking around an idea. I probably shouldn't mention it to you without talking to Aunt Ellen and Uncle Ray first, and to the Mooneys, but I don't think any of them would object, and your morale could use a boost."

He paused. I couldn't guess what was coming.

"If you want, you can fly home and stay with the Mooneys for a couple of weeks in the summer, and maybe again for Christmas vacation."

If I *wanted* to? "Of course I want to! Hey, that changes everything! Summer's almost here, and Joey won't have so long to miss me. It's a great idea! It's the best you've ever had."

One of my own took shape immediately. "Let me stay at the Mooneys all summer! Coming back for two weeks is a waste of plane fare. You said it's expensive. And that way Aunt Ellen won't have both me and Karen hanging around the house bugging her and getting on her nerves. She'll have one less mouth to cook for, too, and not as many clothes to wash."

"No—now look—"

"I'll do all the Mooneys' yard work and take care of our yard. And Chappie'll have extra time to get more jobs."

My father shook his head. "Two weeks is tops. Take it or leave it. I have misgivings about asking the Mooneys to let you stay that long."

"But they *love* having me there," I argued. "Do you know what Mr. Mooney said in a letter he wrote me? He said I'm generous, brave, and honest. He said I remind him and Mrs. Mooney—"

"Take it or leave it, Gary," he said firmly.

I told him I'd take it, although I didn't see what the big deal was between two weeks and three months. And I suddenly wondered why he'd gotten this idea only yesterday. He could have saved me a lot of grief by getting it earlier.

He glanced at me and asked, "Do you think I'm a bad father?"

The question jolted me. Recently, I'd pretty much condemned him. But deep down I couldn't bear to think he wasn't a good father, and I didn't want him to think I did. "You're not a bad father," I told him.

"People will think I am if you go around cursing."

For a moment I wondered where this had come from. Then I remembered. "I hardly ever do," I said defensively. "Just with guys. You know."

He took his hand from the wheel and placed it on my knee. "I do know. And I love you. I love you very much."

Oh, God. I hated this. "Me too," I mumbled, staring at his hand.

"You love yourself?"

"That's *not* what I meant."

"Then what did you mean?"

I could tell he was finding this very funny. Gruffly, I said, "You know."

His hand squeezed my knee. "That's right. I know that, too. I know everything about you. I have a window on your mind."

As his hand left my knee and went to the radio dial, I protested, "You think you do, but you don't."

"Yep. I do. It's better than watching Star Trek; better than reading Homer." Turning the dial, he scrambled commercials and music into a mess of noise. "Now, if I can find a station we both can tolerate, I'll be a real wizard."

So, we'd gotten past anger and love and could relax the rest of the way to the airport. My father wasn't one to tense up in heavy traffic, or get nervous about having to be somewhere by a certain time. He'd stopped the dial at an easy-listening station. The music made me think of cottage cheese being mashed into my brain.

In the busy airport terminal, we sat beside each other killing time. He said he would call me often, and he would call the Mooneys frequently to see how Joey was. Then he leaned close to me and said, "I'm glad you're not scared about going away, because I sure am."

"You're scared of going to Japan?" I asked, interested and surprised.

"You bet," he answered. "I'll be in a strange place where people do things differently. They might see me as some sort of imbecile. Or they might resent me for having knowledge they don't have. As hard as I try to please and fit in, they might not accept me. My only friend for a whole year could be my face in the mirror. 'Hey—great to see you.' I'll say to it every morning. 'Want to brush our teeth together? After that, we can shave.'"

I chuckled, but I'd recognized some of my own fears, which I hadn't told anyone.

"What it boils down to is that in Japan I might fall on my face and stay that way for a year."

"Then why did you say you'd go?" I asked. "You didn't have to." He was leaving the next day. His suitcases were packed and by our front door. But if he felt so strongly about it he could still change his mind, and we could both remain at home without it being my fault.

The moment I came to this realization, a pounding started in my chest, and the blood rushed in my ears. It could happen: my dad and me shooting up from our floor-bolted chairs and shouting, "Hell, no! We won't go!" We'd plow through the crowd to get out of the building and be back on the freeway in minutes, bound for home and Joey.

"Partly it's for my career, and your future," he said.

Turning toward me, he leaned close, and I could smell both coffee and Listerine mouthwash on his breath.

"The other part is the challenge. When I feel I might not be man enough to meet it, I think of you when we gave you Joey. You were so terrified of dogs, you'd have run from a Chihuahua. So what happened when we surprised you with a German shepherd puppy weighing twenty-five pounds? You swallowed your fear and met the challenge. I almost burst with pride that morning. Your mother felt the same. And whenever I'm confronted with one of life's big hurdles, that's my inspiration. You with Joey."

When he stopped talking, I was blinking tears. As fresh in my memory as if it had been yesterday was the moment when Joey first rested his head on my lap and, by ignoring all else around him, let me know that I'd become the center of his world.

"Do you remember that day?" my father asked.

"Yeah, I guess." I squinted as if trying to visualize it. Then my flight was announced. We and those around us stood and turned toward the door, as people in a movie theater do when the movie has ended.

"Got your ticket?" my dad asked needlessly. I showed it to him. A line was forming. We shook hands. The act, instigated by him, made me feel foolish. But then he opened his arms. I sank into him, my face by his throat. I felt his body nearly the whole length of mine and wasn't embarrassed.

We broke apart. His eyes looked moist. Mine were steaming, although—and this seemed miraculous—I didn't spill a

GRANDMA LOUISE SAYS OUTRAGEOUS THINGS

single tear. His voice was thick when he said, "I'll talk to the Mooneys this afternoon about your coming to visit. If they say it's all right, I'll call your aunt and uncle and square it with them. Don't say anything about it before I do."

I said I wouldn't. My flight was announced again. He wanted another hug. I felt reluctant this time but tried not to show it. With his lips close to my ear, he softly said, "What Mr. Mooney said you are, you are."

He let me go. I turned away to grab my carry-on stuff. "Don't forget to eat when you get to Salt Lake City," he said. "You'll have plenty of time."

We'd been over this twice. I said, "I won't forget."

"Okay, champ. Goodbye."

It was my first plane trip. The seat numbers confused me as I made my way down the aisle. I thought I would walk past my seat, which would be embarrassing, and I was relieved when it didn't happen.

I was by a window facing the terminal. I looked for my father but couldn't see him. He was there, though; he'd told me he would stay until the plane took off. If he'd located me in the row of dark windows, he would know by my expression that I couldn't see him and that I felt bad. So I smiled and waved, then turned from the window.

I was buckling my seat belt when I realized that my chest was heaving and I was going to cry. *Buck up old chum. It'll all be ducky after tea.* Two silent recitations of my former teacher's words got me past the moment dry-eyed.

One thing I didn't worry about on that flight or the next one was how I would get along with my Uncle Ray. I'd seen my aunt and uncle twice since my mother died. They'd stopped by Long Beach and stayed with us after vacationing in San Francisco when I was twelve, and on their return from a Hawaiian vacation when I was thirteen. Karen hadn't been

103

with them either time, so Joey being in the house was no problem. Uncle Ray even played with Joey during the more recent visit, getting down on his hands and knees in the living room one afternoon, and chasing Joey into the hall. When Uncle Ray came crawling back, Joey was chasing him. Aunt Ellen—when she could stop laughing—said she'd never seen anything so funny.

I'd liked my uncle during those brief visits and had been very interested to hear him talk about Karen one evening when he didn't know I was listening. It happened the same day he played with Joey. I'd been on my way from my room to the living room, where the adults were drinking cocktails. Uncle Ray's voice carried to the hallway when he said, "Karen's at an awful age. Girls at thirteen are the pits."

I knew Karen's behavior wouldn't be discussed purposely within my hearing, so I stopped in the hall.

"I love my daughter terribly, but she can make me wish she'd never been born," said my uncle.

Aunt Ellen admonished, "You don't mean that."

"You're right," he said. "I wish she'd been born to another family—in Nebraska.

"Too close," said Aunt Ellen. "Try Iowa."

All three burst into laughter.

When my connecting flight from Salt Lake City ended at the two-gate airport east of Rapid City that afternoon, I wondered what Karen was like now. She might be all right. People did change for the better sometimes; Uncle Ray was an example of that. Anyhow, I'd know soon.

It was snowing. Through my window, I saw it come down. Some of the passengers who filled the aisle leaned down to peer at it through the windows. "Pure powder," said one.

I decided to be the last one off the plane, but when a man in the aisle motioned for me to cut in front of him, I didn't know how to refuse. "We've got some snow," he said over my shoulder.

I'd experienced snow twice before, during winter weekends spent at Lake Arrowhead in the southern California mountains.

Both times it was on the ground when I got to it. Hard-packed and crunchy, it had provoked in me a sense that it was only for fun, almost not real; something to be used and then left behind, forgotten.

"Brr, it's cold," said one of the stewardesses stationed by the door. I stepped outside. The coldness hit me in the face. Snow fell on my eyelashes and nose. It was weightless but affected me like a heavy hand on my shoulder. At the bottom of the metal stairs, I walked forward a few steps and then stopped.

"Get inside before you freeze!" yelled a man hurrying past.

Get inside, I echoed to myself, but I didn't want to be inside with Aunt Ellen, Uncle Ray, Cousin Karen, and possibly Grandma Louise, who was Aunt Ellen's mother. (I'd been told in a letter from my uncle that I, too, would call her Grandma Louise, and that I would get a kick out of her because she says off-the-wall outrageous things.)

My expectation of their smiles chilled me more than the snow. I was the stray, the urchin who had come to South Dakota for want of anywhere else to go. But I hadn't had to come, I thought with regret. One word to my father when we were on the freeway, and he would have driven us home—where we would have remained. Or, I could have asked the Mooneys to get my father to let me spend the year with them. Or, if my mother hadn't died, we'd have gone on as we were; my father would still be teaching and coaching tennis at Wilson High School.

That blame for my suffering could fall to my mother was a new and novel idea. I carried it into the airport terminal, where I was greeted by about fifty cheering people who waved pennants printed with WELCOME, GARY!

Aunt Ellen broke from the crowd and engulfed me in a hug. Then Uncle Ray wrapped his arms around me like a big friendly bear and said, "Wow! I can't believe you're finally here! Have we ever looked forward to this day!"

When he let me go, introductions began, although I noted right off that the few teenagers who had been dragged out by their parents to meet me held back.

"Don't try to remember names," said a man called Warren. A woman shouted at me through a wide smile, "We ordered up snow just for you! I'm Myrna, your uncle's bookkeeper."

I smiled stiffly and shook hands vacantly and articulated "Hi," and "Nice to meet you, too," at people who identified themselves by their relationships to my relatives.

"I've been fishing with your uncle going on fifteen years."

"I volunteer at the Girls' Club with your aunt."

"I'm the mother of Karen's friend Susan."

"Where's Karen?" I heard Uncle Ray ask, and when Aunt Ellen said that Karen was in the restroom, he said disgustedly, "I told her I wanted her here when Gary arrived. Can't she ever cooperate?"

Finally, as we waited for my suitcases to appear on the carousel, people started leaving, saying goodbye to me first, or not. They'd see me again, they said. I'd have supper at their house as soon as I'd settled in. Their son would take me around to meet the other kids.

A kid who had slouched against a wall through all this now ignored his parents' desire to leave, and came up to me. Stuck through his longish brown hair was a WELCOME, GARY! Pennant. "Jake Jackson," he said. "We'll be neighbors."

The toothpick in one corner of his mouth rolled to the other. Our eyes were on a level. I said my name, being careful not to look too enthusiastic. If I didn't screw up, he would be my friend.

Suddenly I was being held around my waist and lifted off the ground. A female voice shouted, "Hey, cuz, how's it going?" Karen swatted me on the rump after setting me down. Embarrassed enough to die, I pretended nothing had happened and didn't even turn to look at her.

"Hey, you mad?" she asked. "Aw, don't be, little cuz."

Jake and I locked eyes in silent understanding. He hated her, too.

In the five years since I'd seen my cousin, she'd become great looking. I could tell by the clothes she had on that day—especially the skin-tight jeans and bulky black jacket—that she wanted to attract attention. That wouldn't be hard for her to do. Every part of her looked good. You wouldn't have wanted to turn away from so much prettiness, if such a hideous personality didn't go with it.

In the airport, Uncle Ray bawled Karen out for staying so long in the restroom, but by the time we were in front of the terminal, loading my suitcases into the back of a rust-brown Ford Bronco, everything was fine between them.

"Daddy"—she called him when she wanted something from him. "Daddy, if I go to Minot with you in June, can Susan come? Please please please Daddy?"

"We'll see," he said, but she squealed happily as if he'd said yes.

We got in the car. In back with me, Karen teetered on the very edge of the seat and thrust her face close to her father to plead, "Daddy, can't Gary share Grandma Louise's bathroom instead of mine? Grandma said she wouldn't care, and Mom said it's up to you. I'm begging you, Daddy. Please?"

Silently, I begged him, too. I'd had many reasons for not wanting to come to Keystone, but hadn't considered the horror of sharing a bathroom with Karen.

Aunt Ellen looked over at Uncle Ray and asked, "What do you think? Your mother wouldn't mind, and it might help keep the peace."

"It's not a good idea," he said.

"I guess not," she said, and then: "No, you're right. We'll keep it the way we'd planned."

Karen scrunched up her face and went through all sorts of body motions to show how angry and abused she was, but a few seconds later she was at it again. "Daddy, if I do good on the make-up social studies test will you take me off sleepover restriction?"

"'If I do well,'" he corrected.

"All right. If *you* do well. Will you, huh? Huh huh huh?" She bounced on the seat with each *huh*.

"Failing two social studies tests isn't a joke, Karen," said Aunt Ellen.

"I know it isn't, and I was talking to Dad," answered Karen, which made Uncle Ray jump on her for being a smart-mouth. He was so furious, although he didn't yell, that Aunt Ellen had to tell him to calm down. He fell silent at last. We all were silent. I wondered if my dad would have sent me here if he knew what went on in this family, and I fantasized making a tape of them fighting and sending it to him.

Aunt Ellen spoke first. "We're not always like this, Gary. I promise."

"We're worse," said Uncle Ray. But he didn't sound angry anymore, and next he said, "All right, Karen. If you do well on the test you'll be off restriction."

She carried on as if he'd handed her a wad of cash and his charge cards. What a sucker he was, I thought, but I hoped she would pass the test.

Karen constantly changed moods on that drive to Keystone. From sullen silences she erupted into happy chatter, and when she was cheerful she was also nosy. She asked me about things that were none of her business. I answered the questions so Aunt Ellen and Uncle Ray wouldn't think I was rude.

I said yes when asked if I had a girlfriend at home, and thought longingly of Chappie.

"Who's taking care of your dog for you?"

"Our neighbors," I said, and realized I missed the Mooneys, too.

Aunt Ellen turned to ask, "How is Joey? Is he doing well on his medication?"

"Yeah, I guess."

She winked, and I remembered our conversation in the backyard on the night of my mother's funeral. I said, "He only seizures once a month. That's pretty good. Dr. Meiners, the veterinarian we go to, says some people would give anything to have their dog seizure just once a month."

"And some would have it put out of its misery," said Karen.

"Karen!" Aunt Ellen fixed her with a fighting-mad stare.

"What? What'd I say? That some people wouldn't want their dog to suffer? Geez—"

"Never mind," snapped my aunt. "Stop taking your anger at Daddy and me out on Gary. He's had a long, tiring day."

"Hey—did I tell Uncle Lawrence to go to Japan?"

"Karen, shut up," ordered Uncle Ray. "Keep quiet until we get home or you'll be on telephone restriction for a week."

She curled up with her face to the window. It had stopped snowing, and it was dusk. I looked out my window at a flat and desolate landscape. Wherever a house or other building stood, at least one truck was parked nearby.

"It's beautiful, isn't it, Gary?" asked Uncle Ray, his voice quiet and proud.

"Yes," I answered.

"Let's put music on," said Aunt Ellen. "Gary, do you like John Denver?"

She sounded hopeful. "Sure, he's great," I lied. I felt sorry for her, and for Uncle Ray. What rotten luck that their good child died instead of their nasty one.

Uncle Ray cut through Rapid City to reach the highway that led to Keystone, and then we climbed, first through stretches of ranchland and rolling hills, then through what I thought was a pretty serious mountain pass. John Denver warbling about getting high in the Rocky Mountains had been followed by The Eagles singing Peaceful Easy Feeling. Karen had fallen asleep. I looked over at her once and wondered how it was that girls could be so pretty and so awful at the same time. Some girls in my school at home were like Karen. I never had anything to do with them, but remembering them made me miss my friends and teachers, and the school itself.

On the plane, I'd made a plan. I would go home for two weeks in August, to keep my second separation from Joey from being horribly long. But I was so homesick already, and I so dreaded living with my cousin, that I decided to go in June instead. And when I got there I'd beg the Mooneys to get my father to let me stay with them until he came home from Japan. If he said no, then Joey and I might have to run away.

"Keystone—gateway to Mt. Rushmore," said my uncle proudly. A minute later, when he stopped the car, Karen wakened full of talk and energy and, against her mother's protests that she would hurt herself, lugged one of my heaviest suitcases inside.

The two-story house we'd come to seemed cut off from the world. Of natural wood and framed by evergreen trees with inches of snow on their drooping branches, it was on the side of a hill, near no other houses I could see.

"Jake Jackson lives up there, around the bend," said my aunt.

Around the bend. How strange that sounded. Everything was strange. I suddenly realized how natural it was for houses to be close together in facing rows, and how unnatural for them to be "around the bend." I was used to exteriors of painted wood and stucco, and interiors that were painted and wallpapered. Throughout my relatives' house, all walls and ceilings were of natural wood. It was like looking at trees that were somewhere between alive and dead.

There were no coverings on the windows, which in the dark of evening looked cold and gloomy. Wherever there weren't hardwood floors, there was light brown carpet. Downstairs, the upholstered furniture was in shades of brown. The kitchen appliances were a rust-colored brown similar to my uncle's car.

Two fireplaces in the house, one in the living room and the other upstairs in my aunt's and uncle's bedroom, were faced ceiling high with dull black stone. Also on the second story, Uncle Ray had an office with black leather furniture. There were touches of black elsewhere. Other colors existed in the house, but that night I saw mostly brown and black.

A large black rug with a geometrically-patterned tan border hung broodingly on a wall in the living room. Uncannily, it was the same black and the same tan as Joey.

"That's from our trip to Greece," said my aunt, seeing me eye the rug. She then went to the kitchen to get things ready for dinner. Karen had already gone upstairs to her room after promising to come down in a minute to help her mother.

My uncle and I went to the room I would use until June. I was *not* staying longer than June.

My room, which had been newly furnished just for me, was on the first floor. It had been added to the house, as had the bathroom—Karen's and mine—next to it, and had an outside door. I hoped Karen wouldn't go through my room to the yard. Uncle Ray, guessing this concern, said, "Don't worry about your privacy. No one needs to use that door. There's another in the kitchen." He said I didn't have to unpack everything that night unless I wanted. "Maybe you should wander through the house some more and get the feel of it," he suggested. He then said, "I'll go upstairs and wake Grandma Louise. She naps before meals."

I'd forgotten about her. Not knowing what to do with myself, and feeling completely alien, I followed him back to the living room. Opposite the wall with the Greek rug, a staircase slashed a longer wall into triangles of light and dark brown. Near the bottom of the stairs, which my uncle took two at a time, was a wheelchair. My father had told me that Aunt Ellen's mother used a wheelchair. Since it was down here and she was up there, I expected Uncle Ray to come down the stairs carrying her in his arms.

He came down alone and reported, "She'll be down in a few minutes." I widened my lips, as if caring. My interest in Grandma Louise began and ended with how she would get down the stairs.

She did it on her behind! It was incredible to witness. This old woman with white hair and glasses appeared at the head of the stairs sitting in a wheelchair. Slowly, she got up from the chair, wrapped her arms around the top of the handrail, and eased herself to the floor. Then she came bumping down the stairs on her butt.

She wore floppy brown slacks, a man's flannel shirt, tennis shoes without laces, and mittens. Red mittens—in the house. I stared, transfixed by this craziness.

When she was about halfway down, she peered at me through the wood rail and said, "You look like your father. I look like mine, too, although I used to look like my mother, and she was a beauty."

Following that information, she continued her journey, using her mittened hands expertly as she eased from step to step. And all the while she went on talking. "Age makes hens of roosters and vice versa. It's true. Men start looking more like their mothers when they get old. They get very bosomy, too. Women grow hair on their chin and their noses get masculine looking. And men's features get soft and feminine looking. In both sexes the voices go to hell. It's all very lamentable but can't be avoided unless you die."

She paused when she had one more step to descend, then said, "Don't worry about it yet, though. Right now you look just like your father, and you're handsome. My word, you are handsome."

Uncle Ray, laughing lightly, threw me a "What did I tell you?" look. Then he leaned forward and slipped his hands under his mother's arms and lifted her to her feet. He helped her into the chair. I watched his face and saw so much affection there. The way he was with his mother reminded me of the Mooneys, although they were husband and wife. But if he liked his mother so much, why didn't he help her down the stairs?

Grandma Louise answered that for me as she removed her mittens and tucked them into a leather pocket attached to the side of the chair. "I get exercise going up and down the stairs," she said. "I have two wheelchairs, plus a pair of crutches in the basement, because the arthritis in my legs is so bad it hurts to walk. But I do stairs, in my fashion."

"You do stairs great," said Uncle Ray. "If they added stairs to the Olympics, you'd get the gold."

Karen came out of the kitchen carrying a basket of dinner rolls. "Foods on, gang," she announced, followed by, "Hi, Grandma Louise. Have a good nap?" Then, without waiting for an answer, she disappeared.

Grandma Louise wheeled herself into the kitchen, and Uncle Ray and I slowly followed. She spoke to me while in motion, her head tilted back. "You call me Grandma Louise, too, Gary. Don't get shy about it and speak to me without calling me anything. My son-in-law in Florida did that for seven years, and I hated it. Grandma Louise. That's my name in this house."

"Uh—all right," I said.

She stopped suddenly, turned in the chair, and said, "You must be mad as blazes that you had to come here. Am I right?"

My eyes went instinctively to Uncle Ray. I sensed that he had a bigger stake in my answer than she did. But I directed my words at her. "Uh, not really. I just wish I hadn't had to leave my dog."

"That's got to be tough," said my uncle, sounding sincere.

Grandma Louise, still in her twisted around position, said, "It's better than a poke in the eye with a sharp stick."

Uncle Ray chortled. "I hope it's a lot better than that," he said, flinging an arm around my shoulders. "For us, it's great. I mean that, Gary. It's wonderful having you here."

I felt grateful to him, and sadder than I'd been, and angry, too, although I didn't know why his being happy should upset me. The mixture of emotions, my tiredness, and the smell of cauliflower—a vegetable I absolutely hated—combined to make my stomach uneasy.

"Jake's mother bought too much cauliflower and gave us some," said Aunt Ellen, bearing a steaming bowl of it to the kitchen's big round table, where I was seated between Uncle Ray and Grandma Louise. "I hope you like it," she said, smiling at me.

"Sure," I said, realizing too late that now I had to eat it. But when the foul-smelling mucous-white stuff was passed to me, I knew I couldn't. And I couldn't admit I'd lied. After a silent practice I said, "You know what? I don't feel so well. Would it be all right if I skip dinner and go to bed?"

The three adults expressed concern but didn't try to keep me at the table. Aunt Ellen said she was glad that my new school wasn't expecting me until Tuesday. "I'd go anywhere in the world if I could get a day off school," Karen said.

I did go to bed, and very soon was asleep, but I woke before midnight feeling wretchedly ill. I went to the bathroom and vomited into the bowl. This had never happened to me before, at least not within memory. The experience was devastating. After dragging myself back to bed, I stayed awake feeling crummy and thinking about Joey. He would cure me if he were here. He would have cured me before I knew I was sick—so I wouldn't have been sick. I thought about Chappie, too, and my dad of course, and other things, but mostly about Joey. The rambling, self-pitying thoughts continued until six o'clock, when I heard stirrings in the house and decided to get up.

When I planted my feet on the floor, I remembered my father saying he would leave our house at five a.m. because his plane was leaving from Los Angeles at seven-fifteen. He'd already gone, I realized, and fell back on the bed in despair. It was too late to call him and tell him that being away from Joey was killing me. I climbed back under the covers.

My need of the bathroom finally got me up. When I'd showered and dressed, I went to the kitchen. Grandma Louise was at the table, reading a newspaper. Two ceiling lights were on. Our kitchen at home was sunny in the morning, and lights weren't necessary.

"Cereal's in the cupboard," said Grandma Louise, pointing. "And bowls are in that one, above the toaster. The silverware's in the drawer closest to the sink. You know where to find milk and orange juice."

"Thanks," I said, probably too softly to be heard. It felt funny being alone with her. I'd known that Karen would be at school and Uncle Ray at work, but I'd expected Aunt Ellen to be home.

"I wish we had a morning newspaper," Grandma Louise said when I sat down. "This is from yesterday afternoon."

"Oh," I answered.

She looked up. "Your aunt asked me to tell you that she won't be home until noon or later. She had a breakfast meeting in the city, and after that she has her exercise class."

"Oh," I said again.

"Oh, indeed," said Grandma Louise.

I felt stupid. She returned to her reading. I ate, conscious of the noises I made chewing and swallowing. She looked up again and asked if I liked my bedroom.

"Yeah, it's great," I said.

"It was added to the house so Alan could have a train room. A room just for electric trains. He was too young and too sick, but my son wanted his son to have a train room, so they built it."

I'd gone cold hearing this. "Did he ever play in it?" I asked.

"Call me Grandma Louise," and I'll tell you."

"Grandma Louise," I said weakly.

She cupped a hand to her ear, thrust her chin forward, and said, "Couldn't hear you."

"Grandma Louise!"

"Much better," she said, relaxing her posture. "He played in it, only it was for his father. Alan knew he was going to die, and wanted to make his daddy happy before going. He was very generous, as giving as anyone I've ever met, and so brave that you wondered where all that courage came from."

Her voice became fierce when she added, "He had *so* much courage."

Under the table, my feet felt numb. "Was he honest, too?" I asked.

"Of course he was honest. He was a little child. All little children are honest, even when they tell bald-faced lies."

I was certain I'd irritated her and wished I could explain why I'd asked the question. Instead, I looked down and shoveled cereal—which I didn't want—into my mouth.

"Will you put our dishes in the dishwasher?" she asked, as she began to wheel herself from the table.

My mouth was full. Under her gaze I hurried to swallow. "Yes," I said. "I'll wipe the table, too."

"Good. Do you want to come up to my room and visit with me when you're finished?"

"Uh—all right." Then I remembered I had to call Mr. Mooney. "Wait, no, I can't. I mean, I have to do something."

As an afterthought, and possibly to redeem myself, I added, "Grandma Louise."

"Suit yourself. I'm not going to go up there either. I've decided to go to the basement."

She left the kitchen, and in a few minutes I heard her bumping down stairs, to do laundry, I guessed. Aunt Ellen had said they did laundry in the basement.

I waited until ten (eight, California time), and then called Mr. Mooney, collect, to say I couldn't live in South Dakota, that already I'd spent a night vomiting because of my homesickness.

I rehearsed it while looking out a kitchen window at a landscape made forlorn by shadows. It seemed that everything was shadowed here, indoors and out. Worst of all was the room I slept in, with its shadows of Alan. My generous, brave, honest, and dead cousin—who had looked like me and had used the room to make his father happy. The similarities between us were spooky.

When Mr. Mooney and I were on the phone together, I couldn't say any of what I'd rehearsed. I asked how Joey was. Joey was just fine, he said. Chappie was fine, too. He and Mrs. Mooney were well as could be. And how was I getting along, he wanted to know.

"Um. I'm okay, I guess."

He told me Joey was taking his medicine nicely. No problem getting it down him. "I understand you had snow yesterday," he said.

"We did."

"Do you like it there so far?"

I considered saying it was better than a poke in the eye with a sharp stick, but decided he wouldn't be amused. "Um, it's okay," I said. We exchanged a few more words, said our goodbyes, and hung up.

I went to the train room (never again would I think of it as my bedroom) and lay on the bed, staring at a knot in a ceiling beam. Maybe I would go outside and walk around in the snow, I thought. But what for? Why do anything?

I closed my eyes and lay still for what seemed an hour. When I couldn't stand it another minute, I bolted up so fast I got dizzy. Swaying on my feet, I considered that in less than one day in South Dakota I'd thrown up and had come close to fainting. I could get very sick here, sick enough to die, and without Joey to help me I really could die.

The narrow stairs to the basement were dark, and I couldn't find a wall switch for light. The steps ended at a cement landing that was faintly illuminated from a doorway to the left. No sounds came from beyond that doorway. I stopped twice in my descent, straining to hear. Grandma Louise's wheelchair was still positioned at the top of the stairs, so she hadn't come back up without my hearing her. I began to think she was dead.

I felt frightened, but in that scoffing way in which we anticipate grisly movie scenes. As I turned to pass through the doorway there was in me, too, the hope that *if* I found her dead I would be sent home to California to recover from the shock.

CHAPTER 11

Secrets

Two high windows behind the washer and dryer allowed light into the basement, where ceiling, walls, and floor were a uniform cement gray. Cartons neatly lined up along one wall were labeled on their sides: BOOKS, CHINA, TRAIN TRACKS.

In one corner of the huge room was a small room, painted to look like a shingle-roofed blue cottage with a garden of red and yellow tulips at its base. The cottage effect was ruined, however, by there being one very small window, which was round.

Since I didn't see Grandma Louise anywhere else, and the playhouse (it was obviously a playhouse) was lit from within, I decided she was in there. Other than the scattering of dust motes, as I crossed the room, there was absolute stillness. I hadn't abandoned the notion that the old woman might be dead.

"I thought you'd come," came the voice of Grandma Louise from inside the playhouse, and even though I would not be sent home, I breathed deeply with relief.

There was a short step up to the room, which had a yellow linoleum floor and wallpaper with faded roses. These were illuminated by a bare yellow light bulb in the center of the ceiling. A large bag of see-through plastic, zipper-closed at the top and covered with dust, contained a jumble of dolls. The vacant, permanent smile of a Raggedy Ann doll made me feel queasy in my stomach.

Grandma Louise sat at a child-size pink table. Two metal crutches with circular parts extending from their tops stood propped against the wall behind her. I'd never seen crutches like those and wondered how they were used, but of course I didn't ask.

"There's no sense in owning three wheelchairs," said Grandma Louise, and I looked from the crutches to her pale but strong face. "Besides, the doctors insist that you exercise until you draw your last breath. It's that last breath I worry about, though. It's probably the most devilish exercise of all."

In a voice suddenly quiet, she asked, "You don't have a basement at home, do you?"

"No," I answered.

"And you've never been in one?"

I made a face, as if basements were something suspicious—something smacking of foreignness. "I don't think houses in California have them," I said.

Her posture became more erect. "There are few basements and few attics in California, especially in the arid southern part where you live. Instead of such sensible luxuries as basements and attics, which are typical of homes here, your homes have termites. I find that perfectly fitting, somehow."

She removed her glasses and dabbed at her eyes with a folded handkerchief she took from her sleeve. I'd seen her do this before.

"*This* basement is a delight," she said. "It's unfinished, as you can see, and only used for washing clothes and storage, so it's full of wonderful junk and it's blessedly quiet, even with both machines running."

She paused to dab at her eyes again, and regarded the hanky thoughtfully before saying, "The sounds made by televisions and stereos and telephones are noise; the sounds made by washers and dryers are not. More to the point, this basement has cobwebs in all its corners, *and* it's a walkout."

She seemed so satisfied with the last detail, I couldn't help being impressed, although I didn't have a clue to what she meant. Apparently guessing this, she asked, "You don't know what a walkout is, do you?"

I didn't answer.

Her expression turned exasperated. "You must learn to speak up, Gary. *Ask* when you don't know. *Answer* when you do. A walkout basement is one with an outside door, which is extremely handy if the basement happens to catch fire when you're in it, or if there's fire at the top of the stairs and you're at the bottom. On the other hand, an ax murderer can get in without being heard."

Shocked, I wondered if she knew I'd imagined her dead.

"Don't worry about it," she said. "You're not in California, now. Here, fires are more common than ax murderers."

I thought I should defend California but didn't know what to say.

"Sit down," she said. "I want to tell you my biggest, most carefully guarded secret."

My knees stuck out from the pink chair and wouldn't fit under the table, making me feel tall.

"Your uncle built this room for Karen himself," said Grandma Louise in a way that told me this had nothing to do with her secret. "What do you think of the porthole? It's ridiculous, isn't it? But Karen wanted a ship's porthole, so she got one."

Turning her gaze to me, she asked, "What's your secret, Gary? What is it you feel you must hide from the world even though you don't want to?"

I felt tricked, and judged. She thought I was a stupid and cowardly boy—typical of California boys. "You said you wanted to tell me your secret," I said, showing her I wasn't going to be fooled.

"I do want to. But I want you to go first."

"I can't tell mine." Then, using a firm tone, perhaps an even bold one, I said, "I won't ever tell it. And no one's going to trick me into doing it."

Grandma Louise, unlike her son, was not much of a smiler. But she smiled at me then and said, "That was decisive of you, and I admire decisiveness. Anyhow, it doesn't matter. The secrets of teenagers can't be very interesting, and the secrets of old people with one foot in the grave can't be uninteresting. So I'll tell mine. Wait, though, until I mop my eyes."

She used the hanky. I felt nervous. She talked about death a lot. Maybe she would tell me this house was haunted by Alan's ghost.

"My secret," she began, "which I haven't told anyone, and I'm trusting you not to tell, is that something is terribly wrong with my eyes. Unless I'm mistaken, I won't be able to read much longer."

What a disappointment. She sure was wrong about the secrets of old people. "Go to the eye doctor," I said. "Ask Aunt Ellen to make you an appointment."

She looked sharply at me. "I make my own appointments, young man. And I believe I mentioned that it was a secret."

"It shouldn't be," I said firmly.

"Well, it is, and will remain so, because I'm deathly afraid of anyone touching my eyes. I haven't had an eye exam in years, it's such an ordeal. And what if a doctor said my eyes could be cured by surgery? I'd have to choose whether or not to have it. That would place me right between reason and terror. It's a bad place to be, my young friend. A very bad place to be."

I could understand her fear, but I thought she was crazy not to go to a doctor and get help. Except for total paralysis, or falling from a skyscraper and taking a long time to reach the ground and become pulp, blindness was the worst thing I could imagine.

"I had my eyes examined," I said. "It wasn't bad."

"No? Well, suppose you needed eye surgery. How would you feel about that?"

"It'd be better than a poke in the eye with a sharp stick."

Thinking she wouldn't like what I said, I waited for her expression to show displeasure. Instead, she smiled. "Why can't you tell your secret?" she asked.

I looked down, as if what I had to hide might be seen in my face. "Just can't," I mumbled.

"When I was your age I had a tremendous secret," said Grandma Louise. "Actually, I was much younger than you are—eight, going on nine. That's when it happened, close to my ninth birthday. That secret shouldn't have been told to anyone. I should have kept it to myself forever. But by the time I was your age, I'd told it to many people."

I was looking at her now. She gazed past my shoulder, as if peering into her childhood. I wanted to hear her ancient secret and felt impatient, the way I sometimes did when waiting for Chappie to finish writing a note.

Grandma Louise took too long. We both were startled by the sound of Aunt Ellen's voice, calling from the basement steps: "Grandma Louise? Gary? Are you down there?"

My unhappiness flooded back then, and it shocked me to realize I'd forgotten, even momentarily, about Joey. Other conversations and events similarly distracted me in the weeks after that, but respite was always brief, and afterwards I'd feel as if I'd betrayed my dog.

Each time I saw Grandma Louise mop her eyes as she called it, or watched her wheel herself across a room, I wished I could tell her about Joey's magic powers.

I had a dream that she and I flew to Long Beach to have Joey lick her legs and eyes. But the dream changed abruptly, as they often do. After Grandma Louise and I were on the plane, Joey and I were on the beach without her. I knew as we ran at breakneck speed along the water's edge that Joey didn't have epilepsy and never would. I woke, compared the dream to reality, and grieved.

Karen fought with her parents daily. I thought my cousin created all her problems, some of which had to do with me.

She hated our sharing a bathroom but was furious when Grandma Louise said at dinner my third night in Keystone that Karen should use her bathroom.

"I wanted *Gary* to share your bathroom, not *me*," Karen whined.

"I know what you wanted, Karen, but we're both women. We don't require as much privacy from each other as Gary does from either of us. Besides, it would be silly for Gary to use an upstairs bath when his bedroom is downstairs."

I said, "I wouldn't mind," and sat back aware of what a fine fellow that made me. Smiling at Grandma Louise, I added, "Going up and down stairs is good exercise."

"Why don't you kiss up a little?" Karen sneered at me. "Just leave it the way it is," she snapped at no one in particular. "He shouldn't be the only one with a private bathroom."

"We are going to leave it as it is," said Uncle Ray. "Now, can we go on to another topic?"

Grandma Louise said, "Ray, it's ridiculous for two teenagers to share a bathroom if they don't have to. You may as well put two polecats in one cage when you have two cages."

Karen cried, "No one cares what I want!" She got up so fast her chair nearly tipped over. Her father told her to sit down, but she bolted from the kitchen. We all heard her scream, "I can't stand it anymore!" as she ran up the stairs. Then we heard her bedroom door slam shut.

"I'll talk to her," said Uncle Ray, getting up.

Aunt Ellen looked down at her plate wearily. "Sometimes I feel like I'm in a cage with a polecat." She lifted her head and smiled at me. "Other times, Karen's a darling little kitten."

Never, I thought.

Karen didn't pass the social studies make-up test, so the sleep-over restriction would remain in effect until school was out. I sometimes slept at Jake Jackson's. While ironing something before school one morning, Karen carelessly filled the steam iron from the vinegar bottle that stood beside the distilled water bottle in the pantry. I not only cleaned out the iron that afternoon, but did some ironing for Grandma Louise as well.

A friend of Aunt Ellen's saw Karen driving around Rapid City in some boy's car when she was supposed to be in school. After that, she wasn't allowed to go anywhere, or use the phone.

I got calls all the time. My new school was in Hill City, a lumber mill town, and I made friends with guys there as well as in Keystone. I went out as much as I wanted, although I had a curfew.

Jake Jackson knew things about Karen, including that she put out. Two seniors at the high school where she was a junior had said they'd slept with her. According to Jake, she now went around with a dropout called Doug who was nineteen, lived with his divorced mother in Piedmont, had gotten a Box Elder girl pregnant, and worked part time at a garage in Rapid City.

"I wonder how she found him," I said.

"Like attracts like," Jake replied, moving the toothpick in his mouth. (He was not unique in doing this. Toothpicks were popular in the Black Hills.)

Jake said, "That's what my mom says. Like attracts like. She says it'll be a miracle if Karen doesn't get pregnant before she graduates."

I hated hearing that talk, as much as I despised Karen, but I didn't say anything in her defense and felt uncomfortable with myself because I didn't.

When my aunt and uncle found out about Doug, they forbade Karen to see him. I was in my bedroom when the fighting began, and I opened my door to hear it better. Uncle Ray sounded about to explode when he threatened, "If he comes near you I'll get the police after him. He may be a two-bit punk but he's a grown man, Karen, and you're a minor."

"What are you accusing me of?" Karen cried.

"Your father's not accusing you," said Aunt Ellen. "Boys Doug's age—"

"What age, Mom? *What* age? He's nineteen, not thirty. What do you want—huh? You want me to go out with boys Gary's age? And why don't you ever pick on him? You know why? 'Cause you think he's perfect. It's just sickening you think he's so perfect. Just adopt him why don't you, and then you'll have the perfect kid. Go ahead! Call Uncle Lawrence in Japan and tell him you want to adopt his precious baby boy."

Uncle Ray, still sounding hot, said, "That's ridiculous. And we're talking about Doug, not Gary."

"I'm talking about Gary!" she shot back. "You made the train room into a bedroom for him, but *I* asked for it a thousand times at least. Weren't you listening? No. Of course not. You never do. Never, never, never!"

Aunt Ellen said, "We didn't let you have the room because it has an outside door and you couldn't be trusted not to sneak out at night. You know that's the reason."

Karen said, "That does it. That's just great. My father calls me a slut and my mother calls me a sneak." She raised her voice and said, "Fine! I'll be both!"

I heard her run up the stairs to her room. "Does this ever end?" Uncle Ray asked angrily.

I didn't hear Aunt Ellen's reply. On those occasions when my aunt and uncle let Karen rave and rant, I understood that they were trying to be fair by allowing her to speak her mind. Still, I thought it was stupid of them to listen to her mouth off.

Sometimes Uncle Ray did shut her up quickly. Often, though, especially when he wasn't home, there were shouting matches between Karen and Aunt Ellen, which would end with my aunt crying or sounding like she was choking back sobs. Those were the times when I hated Karen the most. And it was eerie, because when Aunt Ellen cried I disliked her a little, too, and even myself.

Karen spoke rudely to her grandmother, but they never fought. Grandma Louise made comments about her, though, which were usually funny. The one I liked best was that Karen, just to be different, had kissed a cockroach, and Doug had sprung to life.

Grandma Louise made this remark after the night Doug came to dinner. He had remained Karen's boyfriend even after Uncle Ray called Doug's mother and warned that he would take action if Doug kept on seeing Karen.

Doug's ways with girls were well known, so my uncle wasn't just overreacting. A boy in my gym class said to me, when others were standing by, "Hey, Frank, want to bet on whether your cousin gets knocked up before she's a senior?"

Feeling personally attacked, I showed him my fist and said, "Want to bet on whether this comes out the back of your head without passing through a brain?"

"I didn't mean anything, man. Shit. What do I care?"

It was my first brush with a real fight, and the other guy just backed off. Before that I'd been well-liked in my new, temporary school. But afterwards, I was even more popular. I liked myself more, too.

My aunt and uncle changed their minds about Karen seeing Doug, for some reason, and insisted he come to dinner. Karen seemed nervous about it but also happy.

He came bearing a box of candy for my aunt, which seemed to please her, and a six-pack of beer for my uncle, which didn't seem to please him. For one awkward moment, I wasn't sure Uncle Ray would accept the gift. He did not have his customary bourbon and 7-Up before dinner that night, or offer Doug a drink.

At dinner, Doug seemed uncomfortable about eating, as though green salad, fried chicken, mashed potatoes, and steamed carrots were foreign to him. Aunt Ellen and Uncle Ray tried hard to make conversation with him, but Grandma Louise didn't bother.

Aunt Ellen asked, "Well, do you have any pets?" She smiled at me, then added, "Gary has a German shepherd back home."

Doug said, "I had a dog."

"Oh, what kind?" asked Aunt Ellen brightly.

He studied his knife this time, as if seeking the answer to her question in the greasy blade. "He was part rottweiler and part pit bull. Maybe something else got in there, too, but mostly them two kinds."

"An interesting mix," said Uncle Ray tersely. "Karen, would you pass me the carrots, please?"

Doug shook his head in a way that said there was more to the story. He looked at Aunt Ellen and said, "Bludgeon—that was his name?—he got into my aunt's chicken coop and killed a bunch of chickens so I had to shoot him."

Grandma Louise rolled her eyes. Karen, without turning her head, glanced at her father, who, wearing an expression I couldn't interpret, spooned carrots onto his plate.

Aunt Ellen sighed and said, "I grew up with a Labrador retriever. Sergeant was a beautiful dog, although not as handsome as Gary's Joey. He's the best-looking dog I've ever seen."

No one responded, and it seemed that her compliment to Joey had ended the talk about dogs. My aunt asked Doug if he would like seconds of anything, and told him not to be shy. When he declined, she asked, "Would anyone else like more? There will be leftovers of everything."

Apropos of nothing, Karen blurted, "Gary's dog has fits." Throughout the rest of the meal she didn't smile and acted cold, especially toward her mother.

I became two people in one, the fake and the real Gary. The fake Gary—the only one I let anybody see—was a popular and successful student who acted as if he didn't have a care in the world. The real Gary stared at a photograph of a black and tan German shepherd late at night, had conflicting thoughts about his father, and told no one his feelings.

Letters from Japan and California jammed the Rawls' mailbox. My father must have mailed letters to me nearly every day, so many came. And Chappie's were second in frequency. Both Mr. And Mrs. Mooney wrote often, and I heard from friends, teachers, and even my school principal. One of the girls who used to stick love letters in my school locker now wrote telling me she thought of my cute body every hour of the day.

I answered most letters but not my father's. I imagined myself writing to him all the time; everything that happened at school and at the Rawls' would go into those letters that weren't written. He called me on Sunday evenings, but we never stayed on the phone for more than a few minutes. Why don't you write? He would ask, and I would say I didn't know, that I'd been busy, that I would do it the next day—knowing it was a lie and that I wouldn't.

Every letter I wrote to Chappie, and to Mr. And Mrs. Mooney, included, "Please pet Joey for me." I made no other mention of him.

It had been decided that I would go home in July for a three-week vacation. The Mooneys had asked my father to let me stay with them three weeks, instead of two, and he agreed.

May came, and people talked of approaching summer, when tourists would fill the shops of Keystone, many of which were closed in winter. My uncle promised me that in summer, in the parking lot at Mt. Rushmore, I would see license plates from nearly every American state and Canadian province.

May brought Mother's Day, a celebration I always disliked, with my feelings of unease beginning a few days before the event. At home, my dad would make sure that after we visited the cemetery we had something special to do together. Invariably, the day ended with our having dinner at the Mooneys', with Joey invited, too, of course.

That year, I wouldn't be visiting my mother's grave, or experiencing my father's brave and cheerful loneliness. So Mother's Day, as it came nearer, carried no weight for me. I had a mild curiosity about whether Karen would be nice to Aunt Ellen on her special day; that was all.

And yet I woke that Sunday morning in the middle of May feeling desperately unhappy. The family was going to church, then out to lunch, then on a drive to the college town of Spearfish, where dinner would be at the home of a professor my uncle had grown up with, and the professor's wife, a librarian, and their four daughters, all of whom Karen claimed to loathe.

I could not bear to take part in this day-long outing, I realized, and I sat on the edge of my bed not knowing what to do about it.

My aunt knocked on the door. I knew it was her because she always knocked softly, as if regretting having to disturb me. (Uncle Ray gave two firm raps; Grandma Louise knocked low on the door, and Karen pounded with a closed fist.)

Before calling to my aunt to come in, I got back under the covers, even though I had on pajamas. A Willie Nelson cassette that I'd bought for her for Mother's Day was in a bag on my desk, and I wondered if I should give it to her then or wait until later.

"Hi," she said, her smile and tone genuinely happy, so that I knew Karen hadn't upset her yet. "There's a change in plans. Grandma Louise says she doesn't feel up to going out. I thought I'd give you a choice of staying here with her, spending the whole day out with us, or just going to church and lunch with us and then coming home to keep her company."

I felt certain that my aunt knew I didn't want to go anywhere with them and was giving me this choice—which she would not give to Karen—as a gift. Other things were clear to me as well: Aunt Ellen wanted me with them; Karen might be nicer if I weren't with them, and Uncle Ray, who worried about his mother, would feel better knowing I was here with her.

I sat up and said, "I guess I'll stay here. Aunt Ellen, there's a present for you in that bag." I nodded toward the desk. "It isn't wrapped, but happy Mother's Day."

"Gary, *thank* you." She took the cassette out and thanked me again. How had I known she loved Willie Nelson? She asked.

Her smile suddenly became something else, at least in her eyes. "I wish you had your mother to give a Mother's Day gift to," she said softly. "There's something else I want you to know. You bring us happiness, Gary. You really do. Having you here is the real gift."

I couldn't stand it and was relieved when she left the room. Grandma Louise and I ate breakfast together. She wore a new robe and bedroom slippers, her gift from my aunt and uncle. I hadn't thought of buying her anything and wished I had.

When we were finished eating, she pushed her plate away and asked, "Would you like to hear that secret I had when I was a little girl, and confided to everyone I could get to listen?"

I said I would.

"Well, I was eight, almost nine," she reminded me. "I'd learned recently about death and had been preoccupied by it."

This started me searching my memory for when I learned about death.

"God came and talked to me," said Grandma Louise.

"Huh?" I wasn't sure I'd heard right.

"If by that you meant, 'Pardon me, Grandma Louise, but did you say that God came and talked to you'—the answer is yes. He came to a tea party in my playhouse, which was very like Karen's. That's why I like to sit down there. Anyhow, while I poured, he said, 'Louise, you may choose one person to live forever and ever. Nothing at all will make that person die. But once you've made your choice and said it out loud, it can't be changed. It's final.'"

She paused to sip her coffee. "Ray makes the best coffee in the world," she said, replacing the mug on the table. She took a hanky from a pocket in the bathrobe.

I asked, "You could say it to yourself, and it wouldn't be final?"

She nodded, unfolding the hanky.

In silence I practiced what I would say if God made the same offer to me. God, I choose Lawrence Gerald Frank to live forever. Very quickly and passionately I changed it to, God, I choose *myself*, Gary Timothy Frank, to live forever.

Grandma Louise, finished with her eyes, said, "I could say it to myself, but I didn't. I didn't dare think the words because they might pop out of my mouth like hiccups. I was a child, remember, and children are not always in control of what they say. Anyhow, my first impulse was to choose myself, but because this seemed terribly selfish, I put off making the choice for many years. I told people that God had visited me and wanted to grant me a wish, but I didn't say what kind of wish."

She paused. I said, "They probably thought you could ask for millions of dollars or a stack of gold."

"They thought I was crazy," she said matter-of-factly. "When I married, and became pregnant, I felt glad I'd saved the wish to give to my child. But I had twins, your Aunt Ellen and her sister."

I knew about the sister. Her name was Connie and she lived in Florida.

"Of course," said Grandma Louise, "I couldn't choose between them. Later, the same thing happened. I had grand-children born at about the same time and again couldn't choose one over the other. But when Alan—your poor cousin—was diagnosed with leukemia, I finally made my wish. I said aloud that I wanted my grandson, Alan Kenneth Rawls, to live forever and ever. He died anyway."

She looked away. I was glad not to have to meet her eyes, or say something. She drank coffee again, then said, "The hurt and anger I felt when that happened nearly cost me my life. I couldn't breathe. Light was darkness. I didn't want to live."

I'd forgotten to breathe in the last few seconds, and did now. Then I asked, "God lied to you?"

"No, of course not!" Her eyes looked fierce. "I misheard the instructions, or waited so long that I got it all mixed up in my mind. Anyway, it didn't work."

"Maybe you only dreamed that God talked to you," I suggested.

"Absolutely not. When God talks to you, you aren't dream-ing." She mopped her eyes, then closed them. "I wanted so much for Alan to live," she said softly. "Sometimes, I think that I did it wrong because deep down I really wanted to save the wish for myself. That tortures me. You can't know how much that tortures me."

I reached a quick conclusion; she'd done it wrong for the very reason she'd said. I could think of nothing to say that would make her feel better about it, and she seemed to be through talking. "I'll do the dishes," I said, and got up from the table.

At the sink, I wondered what to make of her story. God didn't come and talk to people! Oh, sometimes—Moses in the desert, that kind of thing. Probably it had happened three or four times in all of history. He *didn't* come and talk to children.

On the other hand, Grandma Louise was very intelligent and too smart to be wrong about anything she saw or heard. And she certainly wouldn't make up a story like that. I didn't think she would lie about anything.

Had some strange chemical managed to get into her brain and cause a hallucination? I just didn't know and never would, I concluded. But *if* God had come to Earth to grant a little girl's wish, the next time he might choose a teenage boy.

Shortly after noon that day, when Grandma Louise and I were in the living room playing Scrabble, and I had my back to the window, we heard a car pull up in front of the house. Intent on finding a way to place my seven-letter word, ELEMENT, on the board, I didn't turn to see who it was until Grandma Louise asked, "Do you know anybody who drives an old green Chevrolet?"

I whipped my head around and saw Chappie getting out of the car. Joey's nose poked over the slightly lowered rear window. "It's my dog!" I screamed.

"You needn't shout. I know it's your dog," said Grandma Louise.

But I was halfway out of the room. I reached the front steps as Joey bounded from the car. He didn't get a chance to jump on me, because I swooped down over him first. He circled my legs, talking to me, telling me with barks and whines and moans that he'd been in agony without me. I turned in circles with him; he made every noise he knew except a howl.

He stopped circling and let me hold him, but his whimpering and moaning didn't stop. I knelt and hugged him around the neck, kissed his muzzle, rubbed my face against his face. He licked me repeatedly and just once nibbled my jaw, hard enough to hurt, perhaps to punish me for leaving him.

Because Chappie was there, I talked silently. "Gosh it's good to see you, Joey. Do you love me, boy? Do you? I love you. I love you more than anything. You're my best friend, my Joey, my Joey boy, my great big Joey boy. I love you so much. I love you and never *never* want to be away from you again."

Panting hard, Joey looked deep into my eyes to see if I meant it. Those honey-brown eyes held me captive; I couldn't look away from them. Besides, everything was choking in me. I couldn't show Chappie my feelings.

She touched my shoulder, then handed me a note that read: Gary, he's had two seizure clusters.

CHAPTER 12

Revelations

Everyone except Karen had been in on the surprise that Chappie and Joey were arriving on Mother's Day. Late that night when I was in the basement with Joey and my uncle, Uncle Ray asked me, "Didn't you suspect something was up—not even when we left you home this morning?"

It did seem strange that I hadn't sensed Joey's nearness. He'd sensed mine. Joey had been asleep in the back of the car but woke as soon as they drove into Keystone, and then he wouldn't stay still or stop whining until they reached the house and Chappie let him out of the car. He was getting more medication now, but as heavily sedated as he'd been, he knew I was near.

The first seizure cluster happened five days after I left Long Beach. The second cluster came ten days later and was more severe. That time, Mr. Mooney and Chappie took him to the vet's. Dr. Meiners called them breakout seizures. They could cause brain damage or death, he said, and although one of several things might be causing them, he was inclined to blame them on loneliness. Joey missed me.

Chappie explained in a note that she was in love with a man who didn't care for her, and since she was going through emotional trauma of her own, she would like to take Joey to Keystone for his sake and hers.

Dr. Meiners thought this was a good idea. When Mr. Mooney telephoned my father, my dad agreed with Chappie's plan as long as she squared it first with my aunt and uncle. My dad even offered to pay Chappie's travel expenses to Keystone, and her first month's rent when she found a place to stay.

Uncle Ray said that Joey could live with us, only confined to the backyard and basement because of Karen's allergies. A few minutes after that conversation, Uncle Ray called Mr. Mooney and asked him to relay to Chappie that a very small but nice cabin was available for rent a half mile from the Rawls' house. Uncle Ray would rent it for her if she wanted.

Chappie wrote all this on Mother's Day afternoon. She and I were sitting at the picnic table on the deck that ran the length of the rear of the house. When she finally finished, she shook her writing hand and massaged her fingers.

Grandma Louise came out to the deck. She stopped at the door, eyed Joey warily, and asked, "He won't knock me down, will he?"

I put Joey in a down-stay on the deck. He didn't break from it—didn't run to Grandma Louise to lick her. That disappointed me, as it told me that he couldn't cure her arthritis, or whatever bothered her eyes. If it were within his limits to do either, no command from me would have stopped him.

This disappointment was not enough to mar my happiness. Not even the seizure clusters could do that. Now that I had Joey back, and Chappie, life was wonderful.

Chappie looked great that afternoon, and was all big, cheery smiles, even when her fingers were sore from writing in that cramped but even penmanship of hers. If she was unhappy about the lawyer, it didn't show.

Grandma Louise, as if reading my thoughts, said to Chappie, "You're stunning. You are absolutely ravishing." Of course she then told Chappie what would happen to her looks later in life.

Joey and I drove with Chappie to her cabin, and I helped carry her stuff inside. A small living room with a fireplace opened to a kitchen the size of a bedroom closet. The bedroom was small enough to be funny. You could hardly maneuver around the double bed, which sagged slightly in the middle, so Chappie climbed over it to pull open the orange curtain. This revealed a bathroom that was hardly bigger than a bathtub, in which were crammed a sink, toilet, and shower stall.

Chappie flopped down backward on the bed and stared at the ceiling, laughing her silent laugh.

Looking at her, I thought how old she was, and I didn't like her age. This confused me. It felt as if something were slipping away. Quickly, I told myself that Chappie looked twenty, not thirty, and that she still was prettier than any girl I knew. Her green eyes and curving lashes were just as I'd seen them long ago. No, Chappie hadn't changed, not at all; only I had.

My desire for her had been innocent until that afternoon when I appraised her, beginning with her age. As she lay sprawled on the bed, I observed how nearly flat her breasts and belly were, and my own chest and abdomen tightened. Her notepad was on one breast. She lifted the pad away and her nipple pushed against her shirt. Without meaning to, I raised my left hand with the index finger extended, and imagined how it would feel to very gently touch that hard, small nipple through the shirt.

With the agility of a cat, Chappie sprang from the bed to the bathroom. I watched as she tested the flow of water from the sink tap and flushed the toilet to make sure it also worked. But before she turned around, I did. I left the cabin feeling ashamed of my penis straining against my jeans, and scared that Chappie would see it and not like me anymore. In spite of my shame and fear, I also felt proud of my masculinity.

Joey and I walked back to my relatives' home, downhill from Chappie and next to Battle Creek, in time for me to have dinner with Grandma Louise. First, though, I made Joey comfortable in the basement.

While kissing his muzzle, I decided that from now on I would sleep with my house key under my pillow in case the house caught fire and flames or smoke blocked the basement stairs. "I wouldn't let you sleep down here if it wasn't a walk-out and didn't have a fire alarm," I told Joey.

Apparently, my aunt and uncle had waited until almost reaching home before breaking the news of Joey's arrival to Karen. She came through the front door screeching at her parents loud enough for me to hear her in the basement. I'd washed the dinner dishes and then had gone back to the basement. When I heard my cousin, I went upstairs to the living room.

"You can't keep dog dander from getting in all the rooms of the house! It's in the air! For your information the air in one part of a house moves to other parts! And what about the laundry—huh? Don't you *care* that my clothes will be full of dog dander? You don't! It's the one thing guaranteed to make me have an attack, and you don't care because you like Gary more than me!"

Karen's stopping to catch her breath gave Aunt Ellen a chance to ask, "Karen, how is it that you can go to other houses where dogs are without getting attacks?"

"When have I done that? I always get attacks but I take an antihistamine and get better. And when I get home I don't tell you about it, *Mother*. Am I supposed to report to you every time I sneeze? I don't *believe* this!"

She whipped her hair around her face, reached out an arm, staggered in the direction of the basement stairs, and cried, "I'll have to take pills all the time if that dog's down there. Is that what you want? Me living my life on drugs?"

Uncle Ray said, "We're just going to see how it works out. If it doesn't work, Joey will stay with Gary's friend Chappie."

Karen turned narrowed eyes on me and said meaningfully, "This Chappie's an older woman, isn't she? What's she doing messing with a kid your age?"

Aunt Ellen said, "She's his next-door neighbor. If you're hinting what I think you are, it's pretty sick, and you can stop it now."

"I wasn't hinting anything! I was asking a question!"

But Karen looked a little worried that she'd stepped over the line. As far as I was concerned, she had. How I hated this bitch whore cousin of mine. Using as pleasant a tone as I could manage, I said, "Chappie's a good friend. She's been our neighbor almost as long as we've had Joey."

"Congratulations," said Karen, her wooden tone mingling sarcasm with disgust. She turned and headed for the stairs.

My uncle predicted her next action by loudly saying, "Stomp, stomp, stomp." But Karen went up quietly and didn't even slam her door.

Joey must have heard all the yelling, and I wondered if it had upset him. Screaming fights weren't something he was used to. When my aunt suggested we all go down to the basement to see Joey, and my uncle said he couldn't wait to see him, I felt glad. Aunt Ellen and Uncle Ray and Grandma Louise would treat Joey warmly and make him know he was wanted here. They would make up for his temporary loss of Mr. And Mrs. Mooney, and my father.

After the women went up to bed, Uncle Ray and I stayed in the basement a long time. We were in the playhouse, sitting on those little chairs. I liked how he kept looking at Joey, who slept soundly at our feet, worn out by travel and the excitement of our reunion.

"He's one gorgeous dog," said my uncle. "Look at that massive head and neck, and the musculature on him."

Joey lay on his blanket from home, on his side with his back slightly curved and all four paws nearly touching. The bottoms of his paws looked wonderful to me—the cushiony charcoal pads smooth in the center and rough at the edges where tufts of whitish hair outlined them. I also liked looking at his identification tag, with his name on one side and my father's on the other.

"I want you and Joey to come with me to North Dakota the week school's out," said my uncle. "We'll just be gone four or five days."

School let out earlier here than in California. It had to do with farm kids being needed at home during the growing season.

"Aren't Karen and her friend Susan going with you?" I asked.

"No. I've decided not to take them. They'd drive me nuts, and they wouldn't like Minot anyway. We'll make it a man's trip."

"Won't Karen be upset?" Not that I cared. She couldn't be more hateful toward Joey and me than she already was.

"I don't think so. Her Aunt Connie's going to invite her to visit Florida, and she'll be too excited to care about Minot. She loves her aunt. They get along real well together."

"Amazing," I said. It just slipped out. Uncle Ray chuckled. Relieved that he hadn't taken offense (after all, Karen was his daughter), I laughed, too, and said, "Well, then I guess Joey and I will be going with you to Minot."

"Good. You'll like it. Minot's the frontier. One of the last. They call it the Magic City. It sits at the foot of the Turtle Mountains up near the Canadian border, and just to the south is Lake Sakakawea. That's a man-made lake that snakes all the way to Montana."

To me, Montana had the best-sounding name of any state. I liked how Lake Sakakawea sounded, too.

Giving me a thoughtful look, Uncle Ray said, "I'll tell you something no one else knows. I've got a desire a mile wide to walk that lake from its beginning to its end. I'll never do it of course, but I can't even think of North Dakota without wishing I could.

I wondered why he couldn't do it, and it crossed my mind that someday I might walk the lake, maybe with my dad.

"The Souris River cuts through Minot," he said. "Souris is French for mouse." He broke into a grin and said, "You've got to love a city that's bisected by a river named Mouse. Another great thing about Minot—it used to be so lawless, in the early days, that when the train pulled into town the conductor called out, 'Minot. This is Minot. Prepare to meet your God.'"

I could hear the conductor's call. I pictured a lawless town where anything could happen, where the moment a boy stepped off the train he was instantly grown up and free.

"Minot sounds good to me," I said.

My uncle reached to touch Joey's tail. "It's not for everyone, though. It's cold as Siberia in winter. Well, let's go up. It's late."

We stood and pushed our chairs in. "I'm glad Joey's here," Uncle Ray said. "He'll be fine now. I've got a gut feeling about it, Gary."

The following Saturday my uncle went to Newcastle, Wyoming. He and his two partners in the western-wear business were opening a new store there. They had eight other stores, five in South Dakota and one each in North Dakota, Colorado, and Nebraska.

That morning, Karen came down to the kitchen wearing black leotards and a scoop-neck, long-sleeved white top that clung to her breasts like a second skin. I saw her nipples and was surprised at how large and dark they were.

Grandma Louise was reading a day-old newspaper and drinking coffee. She looked at Karen, folded the paper on her lap, and wheeled herself from the room.

"My God, where'd you get that top?" demanded Aunt Ellen. "You may as well be naked."

Karen shrugged. "It's Diana's. Her mother doesn't mind it."

"Well I do and especially around Gary. Go change."

"I will when I've eaten." Karen yanked open the cupboard where cereal was kept.

"Go upstairs and change, Karen. *Now.*"

"Hey, who left this almost empty?" Karen demanded, shaking the Cheerios box.

In measured tones my aunt warned, "You are risking your sleepover privileges the whole month of June."

Karen left the kitchen. She hadn't closed the cupboard. My aunt closed it. "I don't know how you stand all this fighting when you're not used to it," she said to me.

"It's probably what most families go through," I said, trying to sound diplomatic. "Anyway, I'm used to it now."

She half laughed, half groaned. "I guess you are." Ruffling my hair as she passed my chair, she said she was going out for a walk.

Karen came back wearing an unbuttoned shirt over the clingy white top. The shirt hid her nipples, which I couldn't get out of my mind.

"The whole house smells of dog," Karen complained while pouring Raisin Bran into a bowl. "Why does Joey smell so strong? Does epilepsy make him stink?"

I swallowed my last mouthful of Cheerios before saying, "Not that I know of. What makes you stink?"

"Watch it, buster. I can flatten you with one hand tied behind my back."

I didn't respond, but I was steaming. Joey didn't smell bad. People always commented on how nice and clean he smelled.

Karen brought her cereal to the table. Even the way she sat down on a chair was angry. She glowered at the window. "Geez, can't the weather ever be decent? It's going to be overcast all day. Doug and me were going to the lake today so we can get an early tan."

Doug and I, I thought. She had two pimples on her chest and another on her chin. I said, "You could smear Clearasil all over and call it an early tan."

"You know, you really are a scuzzy little creep."

"You asked for it."

"Yeah, how?"

"Saying Joey smells."

"It happens to be true. He's got a pungent odor. You're used to it and don't notice."

"I'd know if he smelled."

"Who would tell you? Chappie the friendly neighbor?"

"Yep. She would."

"Don't be too sure. There are lots of things people don't tell you because they don't want the precious little boy to be upset."

"Like what?"

"Like about your family."

"Like what about my family?" By now I wished I wasn't doing this but couldn't stop myself.

"Like never mind." She leaned over her bowl.

"My family's just me and my dad. There's nothing about the two of us that I don't know."

She raised her eyes. They were full of contempt. "There used to be three people in your family, in case you forgot. Your mother? The woman who died and you couldn't be bothered to cry at her funeral?"

I laughed as though amused, but my face was hot. "What about my mother?"

"Never mind."

"Sure, because you don't know anything. You're just trying to bug me. I know things about you, though. Everyone in my school does."

Her expression revealed that my words had stung. Trying to sound nonchalant, and amused, I said, "So, what do you think you know? Something scandalous? Go ahead and say."

Now she looked satisfied and in a mock drawl she said, "Don't hold your breath waiting." She got up from the table, left her bowl and spoon by the sink, and left the room.

I waited a few minutes before getting up. I was trying to think what it was that Karen knew. Something important had happened between my parents, and I had to find out what it was. Had they been unhappy together? Had my dad cheated on my mom? Did my mother get pregnant by another man before she married my dad, and gave her baby up for adoption?

Maybe Grandma Louise would tell me. But I couldn't just go up to her and ask. I would have to approach the subject in a way that would make her think I already knew what she and everyone else knew—that I just wanted to see if her facts matched mine.

I rinsed my dishes and put them in the dishwasher. I took the coffee pot into the living room, where I knew I'd find Grandma Louise. "Want some more coffee, Grandma Louise?" I asked.

"Yes dear, thank you."

"I suppose you heard Karen and me fighting. I sure have trouble getting along with her."

"I wouldn't worry about it. Karen's hostility is like a black widow's web. It shoots off without logic in all directions. It's so tough you can hardly knock it down."

That analogy was so brilliant that I went back to the kitchen repeating it to myself, and forgot my mission to pry information from Grandma Louise.

Karen never stopped complaining about the weather that May, or about Joey. After a warm weekend she planted flower seeds given her by Doug's mother, but she did this against her own mother's advice. It was too soon to plant, Aunt Ellen warned, and sure enough Keystone had frost that night. Karen screeched, "Why does God hate me? Why does he hate flowers?"

Her grievances about Joey were usually whined. I loved when my uncle suggested, in response to her whining that Joey's dander permeated the whole house, that she go from room to room collecting it for evidence. Later, when Karen complained that I constantly carried dog hair on my clothes, and being near me made her sneeze and get hives, Aunt Ellen said, "I'm sure Gary will forgive you if you keep your distance from him."

Actually, Karen did sneeze a lot, especially when she got up in the morning. But I didn't think it was because of Joey, and I never saw hives on her. Once, when I was fixing myself a snack in the kitchen, and Karen came in to get a drink of water, I saw her itch herself in her butt crack. So that was where she got hives, I thought, and I laughed.

She whirled and demanded, "What're you laughing at?"

I didn't answer. With exaggerated calm, and without looking at her, I wiped up the bread crumbs and dribbles of jelly on the counter.

"You'd better watch it, punk. I've got a boyfriend who doesn't like people upsetting me."

"Watch it yourself. I've got a dog who doesn't like people upsetting me."

"Oh? What'll Joey do? Throw a fit and scare Doug away?"

"Maybe he'll use his teeth."

I thought that was a pretty good comeback, and I thought I saw admiration in Karen's eyes. But it wasn't that; it was anticipation of her own retort: "Maybe Doug will use his gun."

That stunned me. I couldn't answer.

Karen singsonged, "Gary the fairy's going to tattle to his Auntie and Uncle that terrible Karen threatened to have his doggie-woggie shot." Her voice turned sour and she said, "Go ahead and tell them. I don't care what you do."

She left the kitchen. I stared at my bread and jelly, then stuffed it down the sink drain and ground it up in the disposal. My hand on the wall switch trembled. I was scared. The principle that makes people believe that a dog who bites once will bite again told me that Doug would kill more than one dog.

I got Joey and walked him the half mile to Chappie's, to report Karen's threat. Chappie wasn't home, but she never locked her front door and we went inside anyway. I took Joey off his lead, and he went right to his favorite napping place at Chappie's—the tiny bathroom.

Sometimes when Chappie had a job somewhere, she would leave a note on the table telling me when she'd be back. There was paper on the table that afternoon, but it wasn't a note to me. "I still love you, Stephen," she had written. "I guess I always will. Isn't that strange, since we never kissed and you never even touched me? Not with your hands, anyway. You just reached into my soul with your eyes and touched me there. Now I'm in the deepest pain from your touch, no less than if you had heaped smoldering coals and ice on my soul. Stephen, I always thought that love would be as soothing as rose petals and bright stars and fine, sleek horses and wispy white clouds. It would have been that way, my darling, if you loved me too. But fool that I am, I still dream of it being that way. I dream all the time of being in your arms, close against you, protected from all harm, filled with the scent and beauty and wonder and joy of you."

She hadn't signed her name, which made me think she would write more. I wanted to crumple the sheets of paper but instead put them back on the table. "Joey, come," I called, my voice sounding strangled. He came to me. I clipped his leash to his collar, and we left the cabin.

The day had turned sunny, but I didn't know what to do with it. Jake Jackson had to help his mom clean out the basement. I didn't really want to be with anyone, anyhow. Nor did I want to walk Joey along Battle Creek, or do anything else outdoors.

I knew what I wanted: to lie on my own bed with Joey at my side, and me not worrying about anything. I wanted my dad to be home and Chappie to be next door at the Mooneys', and having never met the lawyer.

I started slowly down the road. It descended to another, one that turned sharply toward the heart of this stupid hick town, where a taffy shop was a big deal.

I missed Long Beach and the Pacific Ocean. Flatness was what I missed, I realized—the realization accompanied by a surge of wisdom that made me imagine myself lecturing to a roomful of admiring people. Where I came from, I told these rapt South Dakotans, just about everything was flat and straight, which made it all big, even the sky. In Keystone, the sky was always jammed with clouds, making it look closed in, just as the land did.

Everything looked closed in. Everything spiked up and down or meandered or sank down to a gulch. Long Beach was bright and open. The Black Hills were dark and gloomy. The few swimming pools and tennis courts that existed here were mostly indoors. Basketball, because it was played indoors, was much bigger than baseball or football, and caves were a star attraction.

I'd been here less than two months, and already I'd been to three caves.

Where I came from, people went to the beach and had a good time. Here, everyone—even my uncle—hunted. Going into the woods to shoot animals was what they called having a good time. Everyone had guns and said, with toothpicks sticking out of their mouths, "Isn't the hunting great in South Dakota?" But really, they were bored. They were bored and a lot of them had a Neanderthal mentality, and so, like Doug, they shot dogs.

Chappie had been stupid to bring Joey here, I thought. Now he was in real danger. If she'd just let me know about the seizure clusters, I'd have found a way to go home.

Of course I wouldn't report Karen's threat to her parents. I'd never humble myself that way. And I wouldn't let on to Chappie that I knew what a fool she was making herself into over that jerk lawyer. But I despised her for writing that garbage to him. Smoldering coals. Sleek horses. You could puke. Why didn't she just throw herself in front of a train or slash her wrists if she loved him so much?

We reached the house. Not knowing if Karen was still home, I took Joey through the side gate to the backyard, where his favorite resting spot was on one of the picnic-table benches. He jumped up on it now, and I sat down beside him. "At least we get to go to Minot," I told him.

I wouldn't tell Chappie about Minot. We would just leave and let her wonder where we were.

Stuck in my misery on that bench, I thought about Minot. Minot was the frontier, one of the last, pushing out to unexplored territory. When we got to Minot, maybe I would tell Uncle Ray that Joey and I had to take off—follow lake Saska-whatever to the Montana border. He would understand. Envious, he would shake my hand and tell me I was the man he wanted to be, but couldn't.

I imagined myself saying to him, "One last thing before I go. Karen said she knew something about my family—something that people didn't want me to know. What is it?"

I pictured him shaking his head and sighing deeply before answering, "It's a lie, Gary. Just another of her lies. Maybe she envies you too. Not for the reasons I do, but for reasons of her own. I suspect that a lot of people envy you."

Beside me on the picnic-table bench, Joey raised his head to look at me. I petted him. His ears stuck out flat, silky soft. As I skimmed my palm gently over each one, I imagined our walking into Montana—that state with the lonely, far-away name.

The name of the lake came to me: Sakakawea. That had to be an Indian word. I said it out loud, pronouncing the syllables as I thought an Indian would. Then, making my voice like an old-time train conductor's, I softly called: "Minot. This is Minot. Prepare to meet your God."

CHAPTER 13

Did You Think He Was Made Of Stone?

The day before my uncle and Joey and I were to leave for Minot, Karen didn't come home for dinner. My uncle looked tense and my aunt looked worried and Grandma Louise was unusually quiet. As soon as she finished eating, she went down to Joey.

I offered to wash the dishes, but Aunt Ellen said she would. I was sitting on the living-room sofa reading *Newsweek* when the doorbell rang. From three different rooms of the house, my aunt and uncle and I all went to answer.

"I lost my key," Karen said. Wearing shorts and the clingy white top her mother hated, she held a bundle of beach towels against her stomach. I felt like an intruder, so I went back to the living room. But from there I could still see and hear them.

"Where've you been?" demanded Uncle Ray.

"Doug and me went riding around with a friend of his and we were rear ended and that's why I'm late. I have a terrible headache and my neck hurts. I probably have whiplash."

Aunt Ellen hadn't said a word and looked like she was holding everything in.

"Where were you when you had the accident?" Uncle Ray asked.

Karen lowered her head and mumbled, "Coming back from Angostura."

For a second, I thought he would hit her. She wasn't allowed to go to Angostura Lake.

"You're not to leave the house while I'm gone," said Uncle Ray. "Is that clear?"

She nodded. The towels had slipped down. Her nipples showed through the white top, which wasn't so white anymore. She looked drained of her prettiness.

Aunt Ellen finally spoke. "Go upstairs and change, and put what you have on and the towels in the chute."

Karen marched off. Her parents looked after her. "God," said my uncle. Then, to Aunt Ellen, "Do you mind if I go for a walk to cool off?" When he'd gone, she came and sat on the opposite end of the sofa. She didn't speak, and I didn't either. But the pages of *Newsweek* were a blur.

Karen came down in a robe and slippers. She started past the living room. "Come here, Karen," said Aunt Ellen.

Karen stopped in the middle of the room. "What? I can't talk now. I'm going to go get aspirin. Then I'm going to the basement."

"Why are you going to the basement?" My aunt's voice was cold.

Karen sighed exasperatedly. "I accidentally threw my sandals down. And there's five dollars in the pocket in my shorts."

"Joey's down there," Aunt Ellen said.

"I *know*. But I have to get my sandals and money."

"Won't you get an allergy attack? Or is that something you lie about? There are so many lies it's hard for me to separate them from the truth. I don't even know if your neck really hurts."

Karen's eyes flashed anger. "Too bad I only got whiplash and didn't break my neck." She started to leave the room but turned and said to me, "Gary, you're lucky you're you. Can I be you? No, I forgot, you're Alan."

When Karen was gone, I glanced sideways at Aunt Ellen. She'd covered her face with her hands. Her shoulders shook. I looked at my magazine without reading—worrying about Joey being in the basement with Karen.

There was cause to worry. Screams echoed from the basement stairs: "Mom! Joey attacked me! He attacked me!"

Aunt Ellen reached Karen in the living-room entry. "He jumped on me! Mommy, he jumped on me!" Karen flung her arms around her mother's neck. "He jumped on me and almost knocked me down, and he slobbered all over me! He scratched my arm. If I hadn't gotten away he'd have bitten me!"

Aunt Ellen shushed her and led her to the sofa. She cradled Karen against her as if she were a little child. Karen began crying.

I got up. I was trembling down to my feet. Joey had cured Karen's whiplash. This I knew for sure. I turned away from my aunt and cousin and went to the basement.

Joey met me at the basement door, and with eager glances back at me led the way to Grandma Louise, in the playhouse. He sat down beside her and stared at her with self-importance. I could see clearly that he was saying, "Tell him what I did!"

Grandma Louise said, "This amazing dog of yours jumped on Karen and licked her all over the face. Then he jumped on me and licked my eyes. It happened so fast I barely got the first one closed in time. I tried to stop him from licking the other one but couldn't."

She looked at Joey, then back at me. "It was an experience, I tell you."

"Grandma Louise, how do your eyes feel now?" I asked.

"They feel fine. He didn't hurt me. It just took me by surprise."

"But how do they *feel?* Are they better? Not running as much? Since he did it have you had to mop them?"

"Hmm. They are better. That's queer, isn't it? They're not running at all. No, they haven't run since he did it, but that wasn't very long ago—just a few minutes."

I dropped to my knees and put my arms around Joey. To Grandma Louise I said, "They *won't* run anymore, or not as much!"

Then I tried to calm my voice. "Grandma Louise, Joey has the power to cure sickness when it's within his limits. I thought he couldn't cure your eyes because he didn't lick them before, but he must have been waiting for the right time. Or maybe he thought he couldn't do it and just tonight realized he could. Maybe he decided to give it a try after the excitement of curing Karen's whiplash and her headache. That's why he jumped on her. See? He cures bruises and heel spurs and all kinds of stuff with licks. They day we got him he licked my ear and cured my earache, and the day we met Chappie he made a bruise on her knee get well. He's cured animals at the vet's and old men in the park. And when a dove in our yard had a broken wing he fixed it and the dove flew away."

All this came in a rush. When I stopped, Grandma Louise said, "Remarkable." She reached to pet Joey's head, and he leaned forward to make it easier for her. "I wonder if he'll cure my arthritis. No, I don't suppose that's within his limits."

"He did cure arthritis once. One of the old men in the park had it. But it was just in his hands and not as bad as yours."

"I'm sure it wasn't," said Grandma Louise firmly. "It's enough, though, that Joey actually made my eyes better. I'm truly in his debt, and in yours because he's your dog."

I could see she meant it. "Grandma Louise? Karen says she knows something about my family that I'm not supposed to know because I'll be upset. Do you know what it is?"

"No," she answered.

"Did my dad ever do anything bad? Did my mom—"

"Gary, of course your father has done bad things. Did you think he was made of stone? He's human, and to be human is to do bad things sometimes. But he's an outstanding person. He's intelligent and clearheaded and feels about most events of this century exactly as I do. I can't think of a thing I don't like about him. As for your mother, she was a jewel, as sweet and cheerful as she was pretty. I would look into her beautiful blue eyes and see pure goodness. And they loved each other like no other couple I have met. There are no skeletons in your closet unless there's one *you* put there that I don't know about."

I breathed deeply with relief. So much for Karen, the lying bitch.

Grandma Louise asked, "Is Joey's ability to cure illness the big secret you couldn't tell me?"

"Yes. Chappie thinks if the world finds out, he'll be taken away. She thinks scientists will cut his brain open, or he'll miss me so much he'll have a seizure cluster and die. A cluster's when—"

"I think I know what the word cluster means, Gary. I also think people would be more interested in you than Joey if your secret got out. They wouldn't cut your brain open but they'd think you were crazy, and that's not pleasant."

She was right. I felt relieved about Joey, and I didn't want people thinking I was crazy.

Grandma Louise asked, "Would you like me to tell Karen that if she doesn't have whiplash she can thank Joey for it? I'll say it's my own belief that Joey has the power to cure. I won't let on that you even know about it."

"Sure, go ahead." I thought Karen's feelings about Joey might change and then he wouldn't have to sleep down here anymore.

Karen's neck didn't hurt in the morning. She felt fine, she said, coming into the kitchen without putting a robe over her nightgown or combing her hair. I noticed she didn't serenade us with her usual morning sneezing. Besides curing her whiplash, Joey had cured her allergies—if she ever really had them.

Because Karen was all right now, Uncle Ray and Joey and I were able to leave for Minot as scheduled. The morning was overcast. Joey no doubt wondered where we were off to, and if it had anything to do with him. This was to be a business trip for my uncle, but we would stay at the home of Pete Zande, a man he'd known from boyhood and still considered his closest friend.

I'd visited Chappie the day before to say goodbye. I wasn't mad at her anymore, just disappointed in her and a little worried that she'd go back to California to be near the lawyer. I didn't worry that he would return her love. Love happened instantly or not at all, and nothing she wrote to him would matter. How many mushy notes had I received from girls in love with me? Dozens. Maybe a hundred. And not one had made me feel something that wasn't there before, except embarrassment.

With the Black Hills behind us, it was all prairie. We had lunch in a tiny town and afterwards walked around to exercise Joey and ourselves. As we passed a hardware store Uncle Ray said, "I could live in a town like this. Your aunt would go bonkers, though."

I felt about the town as he did. It was so uncomplicated— just some flat streets with low buildings. There would not be surprises. Also, Joey liked walking where it was flat. When he had to go uphill he got pokey. I knew I could live here and be happy.

Then I thought of the ocean, and how, for as long as I could remember, I'd felt that if something terrible were to happen— an attack on America by Russia or an alien power or some new, mutant bacteria—I and Chappie and my father and Joey could escape to the sea. We'd get on a boat and go. It was a margin of safety that I didn't want to give up. I didn't want to live anywhere, for very long, that wasn't near an ocean.

We spent that night in Dickinson, in a motel that allowed dogs. Uncle Ray called home and Aunt Ellen told him that Karen was being very sweet. She'd even styled Grandma Louise's hair.

He hung up looking exceptionally happy. Slapping his thighs, he said, "Let's find a steak joint—one where the fries are fat and sassy and the ice cream sundaes weigh two pounds. Just don't let me eat so much I'll get a stomach ache."

"Don't let *me* eat too much," I answered. How I liked him! I wanted to tell him that neither of us would have a stomach ache very long no matter what we ate, because Joey would fix it, but I didn't.

The following morning we drove under a gray and heavy sky to Bismarck. We walked Joey on the capitol grounds, which were planted with trees from every state in the Union, then headed north for Minot.

"How much longer before we'll see the Turtle Mountains?" I asked.

"Hah!" Uncle Ray exploded. "When you feel a little bump under the car—like we drove over a turtle—that's the first one. Didn't I tell you? They're just low, rolling hills. There aren't any real mountains in North Dakota."

There seemed hardly to be anything in North Dakota except prairie and a sky of cloudless blue. Despite the almost overwhelming flatness of the land, it seemed as if we were climbing to the top of America.

It was on that leg of our journey, on U.S. 83, that I began loving North Dakota. I couldn't have said why.

I couldn't say no to Pete Zande's daughter, Nancy, who was my age to within a week, when she asked me to go down the street with her that afternoon to show Joey to her best friend. The best friend wasn't able to go out for some reason I wasn't told.

The Zandes' house was at the top of a hill from which you could see most of Minot, and, beyond the city, a band of open land that joined the horizon. We walked downhill slowly, although Joey pulled at the lead a little as if eager to explore.

The best friend, whose name was Daphne, was waiting for us in front of her house. She started petting Joey right away, not letting him sniff her first as she should have done. But he didn't mind a bit, and I didn't either, because Daphne, with short dark hair and big brown eyes, was the cutest girl I'd ever seen. Immediately I saw that her personality matched her peppy looks.

"You can bring him in," she said. "My mom wouldn't mind. She loves dogs."

In the kitchen, I took Joey off lead. He followed Daphne around as she pulled Cokes and guacamole from the fridge, and chips and cookies from cupboards.

Nancy and I were on stools at the eating counter. "What can Joey eat?" Daphne asked, smiling at me as she pushed a Coke across the counter. The can kept coming, over the ledge and onto my lap. "Oops," Daphne said. "I didn't mean to do that."

I had Coke from my crotch to my right knee. "It's my fault," I said. "I shouldn't have ordered a double."

Both girls giggled. I felt pleased with myself for coming up with a good quip. But my groin was ice cold and wet, and I was also embarrassed.

I became more embarrassed when Daphne suggested I wear a beach towel while she washed and dried my jeans.

"No, I'd better go back and change." I slid from the stool. Joey had been lying down and he got up too.

"Leave Joey here," Daphne said, leaning over to enfold him in a hug.

"Why?" I asked, thinking it was a pretty radical suggestion.

"Because he's wonderful," she said, drawing out *wonderful.* "He's the most gorgeous dog I've ever seen. And I never ever get to see a German shepherd. All we have in this neighborhood are small dogs."

She rubbed her cheek against Joey's. He was grinning, lapping up this attention. Anyone who tells you that dogs don't smile is wrong.

Daphne said, "Anyway, if you leave him here, you'll come back."

"I'll just be a few minutes." Suspecting that my pants were wet in the rear, too, I backed out of the kitchen. Joey didn't attempt to follow me.

I was on the walkway to the Zandes' front door when I heard male voices from in back. Deciding it wouldn't be proper to go in through the front door when my uncle and his friend were outside, I crossed the lawn and started around the side of the house. Passing a tetherball pole I thought of giving the ball a good whack but didn't.

There was no gate. I was almost at the corner of the house when a question asked by Pete Zande stopped me: "What was his mother like?"

"Beautiful. Tina was a knockout and lots of fun."

I don't know what kept me from continuing on my way, but I didn't. I stood statue-like in afternoon shade. My uncle went on, telling his friend, "She was never satisfied, though. She didn't show it overtly, but there was something in her . . . she made Gary's father start calling himself Lawrence, for one thing. He'd been Larry before they got engaged. And things she said always gave me the feeling that she thought he could do better than being a teacher. He loved teaching. I'm sure he changed careers after she died out of guilt."

"What was there to be guilty about?" asked Pete Zande.

"Not being what she wanted him to be when she was alive. Not giving her wealth and the social status that she might have had if he'd been something else. Maybe that, and maybe . . . ah, never mind. I'm talking too much."

"No, go ahead. Tell me. I'm interested."

There was a pause after which my uncle said, "I've never told this to a soul, and I shouldn't do it now, but what the hell, we go back a long way. And maybe I've always needed to air it, like a smelly mattress."

This was it—the skeleton in my closet coming out to get me. I could stop it by making my presence known. But with a painful tightening in my chest I waited, listening hard for the skeleton's deadly hiss.

"Lawrence was drunk the night of the accident that killed Tina. Maybe not drunk. I shouldn't say drunk. But definitely not sober. They'd been at a big party. You know the rest. Happens all the time, right? It happens *all* the time. That's what Ellen told him when he confessed his guilt to her before the funeral. She said he wasn't to blame, that his car was the one hit, that if he'd been to blame the police would have arrested him. She told me about it when we got home. God, was I glad she didn't do it in California because I don't know what I would have said to the poor bastard. I've done a lot of stupid things in my life, some you could remind me of, but mixing drinking with driving ain't one of them. Anyhow, what Ellen said must have worked because Lawrence got on with his life. I guess he had to, with a kid to raise by himself. But if you're asking me, he changed careers to atone for the drinking he did that night."

Pete said, "Yep, it happens all the time. It's a story told too often and all across the boozy land." Then, with a chuckle in his voice: "Get you another beer?"

I inched toward the front yard, looking down, scared I'd be heard. I'd go back to Daphne's. I didn't care how I looked.

"Hey, guy, what's up?" called Pete Zande.

Knowing he meant me, I turned.

"I saw you from the kitchen. Why aren't you with Nancy and Daphne? Where's Joey?"

Leaning back a little to look past his paunch, he nearly filled the door. Facing this tall and jowly man, I felt physically small and reduced in character to the size of a pea. My uncle, in slandering my parents, had smeared me as well.

"He's at Daphne's," I answered. "I got soda on my pants and came back to change."

My uncle appeared at the door. Seeing me, he smiled. The sight of him stung my eyes. "Where's Joey?" he asked.

"At Daphne's."

"How come?"

"She wanted me to leave him there. I came back to change pants."

"He's got a Coke stain in the worst possible place," explained Pete Zande.

My uncle said, "Joey's outside, isn't he?"

"No, he's inside."

"He shouldn't be," he said with a frown. "Her parents might not like it. You shouldn't take him in someone's house without an adult okaying it first."

Like I'd committed a crime! This goddamn liar had smeared my father's name. He'd called him a murderer, and my mother a snob. "You're right," I said. "I'm sorry. I'll go get him now."

I knew I'd better be cool. Ray had the power to send Joey away. I didn't want that. I had to go on living in his stinking house until I could find a way to get back home, and while I was there I wanted Joey with me.

"No, come in and change first. It's no big deal. I shouldn't have scolded you. I'm the one who's sorry."

As I entered the house, with my legs rubbery and my heart racing, he asked me, "Am I forgiven?"

"There's nothing to forgive," I said, trying to keep my voice from trembling.

He held out his hand. I would rather have grasped fire, but I took it and gave it a firm shake. Like a man—or a coward.

Returning to Daphne's, I saw Nancy coming toward me on the sidewalk. Joey wasn't with her. I went wild in my mind, probably because of what I'd just been through. I thought she'd tell me he was injured or dead.

My anxiety must have showed, for she greeted me with, "Joey's fine. Don't worry."

After exhaling my breath of fear, I asked, "Why didn't you bring him back?" But of course I knew why.

"Oh . . . I dunno." She shrugged, smiling slyly. "Well, you'd better go get him."

I couldn't believe what I saw when I got to Daphne's. She'd changed into a one-piece shiny bathing suit. On a ten-speed bike that she was barely tall enough to handle, she was riding in wobbly circles on the grass around the house. Joey—without a leash and looking like he was having the time of his life—chased her but kept a discreet distance. He barked a few times but quietly, as if knowing that polite guests never make too much noise.

When Daphne saw me she slid off the bike and let it drop to the grass. We faced each other. She was almost straight up and down like a boy, and her haircut, with plenty of thick bangs, was boyish too. Her suntanned skin bore little more color than the cream-white siding on the house behind her. But I felt something I hadn't felt with any girl except Chappie. I wasn't thinking about Chappie, though—not even about my uncle and his lies about my parents. Looking at Daphne, whose last name I'd already forgotten, I really wasn't thinking.

"Was it all right to bring Joey outside to play?" she asked.

"Sure. But you should have put the leash on him. He could've run into the street if he saw a cat or something."

"Sorry."

"It's okay."

"Are you sure? You don't look happy."

Joey nudged my thumb with his nose. I hadn't seen him come to me. My fingers curled around his mouth. "I'm happy," I said.

"Let's go sit on the swingset." Daphne turned to lead the way around the house. Her back was more womanly than her front. Joey and I followed until she climbed onto the wood bottom of a rickety-looking glider. The paint-peeled structure it was part of was missing one swing seat and had rust down the center of the slide.

Daphne said, "We never use this anymore. But my mom doesn't want to get rid of it. She's sentimental."

I stepped onto the glider and decided to sit next to Daphne rather than on the seat opposite. I put my arm around her shoulders. My other hand went to her thigh just above her knee.

"You're a fast mover," she said.

"I'm not," I answered softly, then kissed her. When I couldn't remain conscious without taking a fresh breath, I pulled away.

"I like you," she said.

"I like you too."

"My mom'll be home soon."

"Well, I've got to be going anyway."

We kissed again. Then she went inside to get Joey's leash. I fastened it to his collar, and he and I walked away from her. He looked back, but I didn't.

At the Zandes' I didn't feel quite so small as before. My new hatred of my uncle was less intense, and I was able to meet his glance without difficulty. Watching him in profile as he talked happily to Nancy, I thought: You don't count. You don't exist. You're cardboard. That's all. When you die they can throw you out with the trash. The sooner the better.

But I would not let him off with only my concealed hatred for punishment. No, he must suffer for his lies. I would write to my dad and tell him what I'd heard. My father would order me to leave Keystone at once, and he would put the scumbag Ray Rawls out of his life.

Joey

Joey was allowed to sleep in the Zandes' basement family room with me. That first night, as I lay in a sleeping bag waiting for sleep, I thought over what Uncle Ray had said about the accident. It hadn't sounded made up. And his claim that it happens all the time was true.

I sat up, tightly hugging my chest, squeezing my eyes shut and compressing my lips. I wanted to believe otherwise, but there was no getting around that my uncle hadn't lied. The sheer ordinariness of my parents' tragedy was what really convinced me that my father stood guilty as accused.

Lying down again, I pressed my face against Joey. My uncle's accusation that my mother had made my father switch from calling himself Larry to Lawrence must also be true. In our photograph albums at home, the pictures of my dad before I was born had Larry written next to them.

About my mother having been dissatisfied as a teacher's wife, I had no evidence either way. But she had commented that Chappie could do better for herself than be a handyperson, and she may have said something similar to my father about his teaching career. I hoped not. I felt sorry for him in a way I never had before. The guilt he had to live with was almost beyond imagining. No wonder he never dated.

I felt so much tenderness for my dad that I envisioned him being moved by my feelings in Japan. I saw him shaking with emotion as he stood with head bowed in front of a Buddha statue. Gary knows, he would say to himself, and at first he would think I didn't love him anymore. But that feeling of fear would be replaced by one of relief as he realized—through my *willing* him to realize—that it was all right, that once again I forgave him.

I also imagined him asking if I wanted him to be called Larry and be a teacher again? My answer would be, "Call yourself Lawrence and be a rich corporate scientist to honor my mother's memory."

By the time my uncle and I began our return journey to Keystone, I had stopped dwelling on these things. But of course it was not the same between us and wouldn't be again. He'd blabbed what Aunt Ellen had surely meant to be kept secret. And even though he'd said to Pete Zande that he'd never told anyone else what my father confessed to Aunt Ellen, he must have told Karen. There was no question in my mind that she knew.

I didn't say goodbye to Daphne when we left Minot. Actually, I'd been trying to avoid her because I didn't want to stop being faithful to Chappie.

Only Daphne wasn't willing to be avoided. Besides dropping by the Zandes' on the pretext of visiting Nancy, she just happened to show up nearly everywhere I went. When we met at the zoo, the pioneer village, and the wildlife refuge I treated her politely, but that was all.

She responded with glaring looks and sarcasm. But in a restaurant I caught her looking across the room at me with a hurt expression, and I felt both sorry for her and irritated. Why didn't she simply stay away from me?

The morning we said our goodbyes and thank yous to the Zandes, and drove down their street past Daphne's house, my uncle said, "You won't be quickly forgotten here."

"Why?" I asked.

"Because you broke Daphne's heart."

"I did not."

He looked at me sternly. "My understanding is that you did. Maybe not intentionally, but you did break her heart."

We didn't say anymore about it, but of course I'd known that Daphne was heartbroken. She'd written me a note saying so, and Nancy had delivered it the night before. "I will know better than to give my heart a second time, Gary," Daphne had written. "This is farewell forever from someone you don't care about. But even though you don't care, please don't forget me. Always remember the girl you used and wiped on the floor like an old rag. I won't forget you. I will feel your lips on mine forever."

Girls! They fell in love too easily. One simple thing—in the case of Daphne and me a kiss on a swing, and in the case of Chappie and the lawyer a couple of lunches—and bam, they thought it was eternal love.

I spoke very little to my uncle on our return trip, and he'd lost his exuberant cheerfulness. In fact, I wondered if he knew I'd heard him in the Zandes' yard.

We shared the same motel room that we'd had on our way north. Joey went to sleep on the floor between the beds. At around midnight, he had a seizure.

Uncle Ray woke first and switched on the lamp next to his bed. I leaned over the side of the bed to make sure Joey wasn't hitting any furniture with his legs or head. Uncle Ray said, "Be careful! He'll bite you!"

Ignoring the warning I murmured "Good boy," to Joey while stroking his side. "It's all right, Joey. It's all right." I was lying, of course. I felt sick with fear for him.

The seizure was over quickly. Joey rose unsteadily to his feet. He stood still a moment, then made a dash for the door. I'd already pulled jeans on over my jockey shorts. Uncle Ray was sitting up in bed. "He needs to go out," I said, fastening the leash to Joey's collar.

When the door was open Joey knew right where he wanted to go. He relieved himself on the small strip of grass in front of the motel, then began pacing, anxiously sniffing at the grass and air and me as he went. It was all par for the course. He would work off his restlessness and then sleep. I told myself to stop worrying. Hadn't my father said a hundred times that Joey was strong and could take it?

My uncle came outside. He'd put on jeans and a sweatshirt and loafers. "Aren't you cold?" he asked quietly. "You're barefoot."

Joey was pulling at the lead, going a few feet one way, sniffing and circling back. I said, "I'm not cold."

"I didn't know seizures were so awful," said Uncle Ray.

"That wasn't a bad one. That was mild."

He looked at me, frowning.

"It was less than thirty seconds," I said.

"I see." His voice was weary. He tilted his head back to see the sky. I remembered my dad, on the beach, looking up and comparing the moon to a pie. So desperately did I miss him now, I could hardly bear it.

"Well, come inside now," said Uncle Ray.

"I can't until Joey's over being restless."

"It's the middle of the night. He can be restless inside."

"Just one minute more." I didn't tell him that if I took Joey in now, he would scratch on the door to go out again.

"Gary, let's go in. Joey can walk around in the room."

This time my uncle's tone allowed no argument or delay. I took Joey in. He made one quick tour of the room and then scratched on the door."

"Stop it, Joey," said my uncle

Joey scratched again.

"Joey, off," I said sharply—the first time I'd ever reprimanded him after a seizure. He didn't scratch again, but he paced.

My uncle and I sat on the edge of our beds.

"How long does this last?" Uncle Ray asked.

"Not too long."

"Can't you make him lie down and stay?"

"No. He's got to work it off."

"I've got to sleep. You do too."

Joey was by the closet and just then he lay down. "He's through," I said, hoping it was true.

Switching off his bedside lamp, Uncle Ray said, "Good night."

Joey began panting. I'd forgotten he would do that. The panting became louder as the seconds wore on, or so it seemed.

"Oh, for crying out loud. How long does that go on?"

"A little while."

"We'll *never* get to sleep. Gary, put him in the bathroom and shut the door."

"He'll think he's being punished," I protested.

My uncle got up and carrying his blanket and pillow past my bed snapped,. "I'll sleep in the tub."

After he closed the bathroom door, I wanted to lie down on the floor beside Joey, or call him to me, but did neither for fear of making him restless again.

Soon Joey stopped panting and went to sleep. So did my uncle. I heard him snoring. Lying in bed, I compared his reaction to Joey's seizure to how my dad always reacted. When he was awakened in the middle of the night by Joey having a seizure, his concern was for Joey, and for me, not himself.

Again, that night, I ached with longing for my father. My poor dad. He was human, as Grandma Louise had said, but when he did bad things it was not intentional. He would have chosen death for himself rather than hurt my mom. He would never behave the way my uncle had tonight.

In the morning and through the remainder of our trip, Uncle Ray and I shared very little conversation. Joey's seizure wasn't mentioned.

When we reached Keystone, I couldn't wait to see Grandma Louise, to find out if her eyes were still better. I found her in the basement, in the playhouse. "Yes, my eyes are still better," she answered my question. "I've had to mop them a few times but hardly at all, considering how they were before. Oh—and I did tell Karen about Joey."

"What'd she say?" I asked. "Does she believe he has magic powers?"

"Hmm, I'd say she was torn between belief and doubt. She did suggest something rather provocative, though. *If* Joey really can cure illness, then aren't we morally obligated to take him to the hospital in Rapid City and to every other hospital in the country, so he can cure everyone?"

My answer came quickly: "Grandma Louise, I took him to the hospital when my mother had her accident, and he couldn't help her at all because it was beyond his limits. He got so frustrated that he had a seizure. Most things people go to the hospital for are beyond his limits, and the frustration he'd feel not being able to cure them would make him have a seizure cluster and die. I *can't* take him to a hospital."

She nodded. Her expression said that she understood and agreed.

That night Karen came to the train room. The door wasn't closed. I almost always kept it open, to be better able to hear Joey if he had a seizure. Karen asked me, "Do you think it's right to keep Joey to yourself when right now hundreds of little kids are dying of cancer? In case you don't know, thousands of people are plagued with diseases worse than anything you can imagine."

I was propped up in bed reading. I hadn't looked at her since she'd come in, and I didn't look at her now. She made it sound as if all the sicknesses in the world were my fault.

"People have diabetes so bad that their legs have to be cut off," she went on. "Old people get strokes and can't move or talk the rest of their lives. Don't you care?"

I was too angry to tell her why I didn't take Joey to hospitals. Not wanting her to think that her opinion mattered to me, I said, "Sad."

"Sad? Is that all you can say? You really don't care? Haven't you got any feelings at all for your fellow man?"

I turned a page and said in a bored tone, "Yeah, lots. I want to protect everyone from being plagued by you."

"Very cute. Just think about what I said, okay?"

"Okay," I said to get rid of her.

She didn't leave, just stood there looking at me in silence. Her perfume stank. I couldn't wait to have her out of the room.

"It so happens," she said finally, "that Doug has a friend who's dying of a rare blood disease. He wants to take Joey to him tomorrow. You'll let him, won't you?"

Of all the damn lies! Doug just wanted to get his hands on Joey to get rich. But I wouldn't give her my answer yet. "What do you know about my family?" I asked, still looking at the book.

"Nothing. I just said that to get your goat."

"I don't believe you."

"It's true. One of my friends did it to me once, so I knew it would work. Well, does Doug get to take Joey to see his friend?"

I turned a page and pretended to read the first sentence. I could feel her impatience for an answer. "Doug's not taking Joey anywhere," I finally said. "Not tomorrow or any other time."

She cried, "You'll let someone die a horrible death when Joey could cure him?"

I couldn't keep my voice calm any longer and shouted, "Right! Get out of here Karen and leave me alone!"

"You're a monster," she said. "You know that? God should make *you* die a slow and painful death."

She left. From that moment I didn't stop worrying about Joey. Everything Chappie had warned would happen if the world knew about Joey seemed to be closing in on me. It was my fault, of course. I never should have told my secret to Grandma Louise.

That night, after I had slipped into a delayed and fitful sleep, sounds from the basement pulled me awake. Joey was having a seizure. I ran downstairs.

It was a cluster, and it was awful. One seizure hardly ended before another began. Finally, Joey didn't even try to get up between them. I knelt beside him, terrified, fighting tears, not knowing what to do.

The others had come to the basement and were gathered behind me. The first words I heard were Aunt Ellen's asking, "Ray, shouldn't we get help? Won't Jim Grimes come if you call him?"

"I don't know what he could do," was my uncle's softly-spoken reply. "I don't know what anyone can do."

"He'll be all right," I said, my voice sounding choked. Joey's legs bicycled frantically and his head trembled violently against the floor. "I'll give him more medicine."

"You don't get near his mouth," said my uncle. "That's an order."

Seconds later, the seizure stopped. Something told me, or made me believe, that the cluster was over. Joey's eyes were closed, and his body scarcely moved with his breathing. I bent my face to his.

"Gary!" snapped Uncle Ray.

"Is he dead?" asked Karen. "Oh yuck, he peed."

There was only a trickle of urine on the floor. Saliva clung to Joey's chin and I wiped it off. Aunt Ellen put her hands on my shoulders and pulled me back. "Honey, you must be careful. He could bite you without meaning to."

Joey opened his eyes. He tried to lift his head but couldn't.

Uncle Ray brought a wad of paper towels and wiped the floor. Kneeling to do this, he said quietly but firmly, "Gary, tomorrow morning Joey's going to be put to sleep. It has to be done. You can come with me or not. I'll take him to my friend Jim Grimes. He's a wonderful vet. He loves dogs as much as you do."

My hand on Joey's side trembled and my mind worked feverishly with a plan to keep my dog from being killed.

"Gary," said Aunt Ellen. "Do you want to stay down here with him awhile?"

I nodded.

"I'll get your sleeping bag and pillow, and your pajamas, sweetheart."

I realized then that Karen and my aunt and Grandma Louise were seeing me in my underpants, but I didn't care.

Uncle Ray asked, "You do understand, and agree, don't you Gary? Joey's suffered terribly tonight, and it'll happen again if we don't do what's necessary. It would be cruel to him."

Again, I nodded.

He put a hand on my shoulder. "Want me to stay down here with you?"

I shook my head no. I could play act, but words were out of the question.

"Okay, champ." He gently rocked my shoulder back and forth. "Remember how your dad used to call you that?"

The bastard. I didn't respond. Joey began to move. In a second or two he would try to get up again and I wanted all of them out of the basement before he did. I stroked his side, hoping to soothe him into lying still a little longer.

My uncle was the last to leave the basement. "I've never been so tired in my life," he said wearily. "Gary, Joey's not afraid of dying. He doesn't know anything about that. And he's had a good life, thanks to you." He hesitated before saying, in a flattened voice, "Okay, I'll see you in the morning."

Left alone with Joey I pressed my cheek to his. He breathed deeply now. Reluctantly, because I didn't ever want to stop touching him, I pulled myself away and stood. "Joey, get up," I said. "Get up, my good, good boy."

He rose to his feet so stiffly that I groaned aloud and stooped to help him. His first attempt at walking was equally pathetic. Hugging him—holding him steady on his feet—I whimpered, "You've got to be able to walk, Joey. You've got to."

He slipped down to the floor. Just then Karen returned. She whispered excitedly, "I called Doug and he's going to come and get Joey when my parents are asleep. He'll hide him and you can tell my parents that the seizures made Joey go crazy and he ran away. Okay? Isn't that a fabulous idea?"

"Yeah," I answered. "It is."

"Karen?" Aunt Ellen called down the stairs. "Let Gary be alone with Joey."

Karen left. Joey got to his feet, walked much better, and nervously paced the basement. I put him on lead and took him outside to relieve himself, then brought him back in. It was hard for me not to take off right away, but I felt certain that my uncle would know if I did, and would follow. On the other hand if I waited too long, Doug would come.

I waited about fifteen minutes before pulling off the pajama bottoms Aunt Ellen had brought down for me, and putting on a pair of dirty jeans that had been in the wash. As quietly as possible I opened the door to the yard. A hidden army of crickets clamored loud enough to cover the sound of my heart pounding as barefoot I followed Joey outside.

CHAPTER 15

God, I Want . . .

Joey wasn't up to running. I tried getting him to run just a little, but he stumbled. He tensed at every sound and his expression was confused and suspicious. Sometimes he stopped walking and had to be coaxed into continuing. When our eyes met he looked as if he knew something horrible had happened to him and feared it would happen again.

"Joey, hurry," I whispered once when he lagged, and he looked up at me in a way that made me think he didn't know who I was. Was he brain damaged? He couldn't be! Then the worst happened. He went down and wouldn't get up. I begged and pulled but he wouldn't budge. "Get up!" I hissed through clenched teeth, and still he didn't move. He just lay there staring off toward the woods.

Joey weighed a hundred and thirty pounds. I couldn't lift and carry him. "Get up," I ordered again, trying to pull him up by his collar. He wouldn't. Across the world to my father, in a voice breaking with despair, I pleaded, "Dad, please please please help Joey and me."

Joey stood and began walking but was so wobbly that I thought he couldn't possibly stay on his feet. He had to, though, and I stayed close to him so I could grab him if he seemed about to collapse. It was hard to watch him while also watching where I was going. Constantly, I listened for a car coming up behind us. We would disappear into the woods if necessary.

Before we were in sight of the cabin, Joey picked up speed. He knew where he was going, I felt, and was reassured.

A car I didn't recognize was parked outside Chappie's cabin. I crouched behind it, keeping Joey close beside me. A light was on in the front room. Chappie always kept the window open with the curtain pulled away, so I was able to see inside.

A man was with her. They stood facing each other and he had his hands on her shoulders.

I knew that this was the lawyer. Joey whimpered and strained at the lead. Nervously, I wrapped my fingers around his muzzle to quiet him, but he broke free of my hand and cried louder. I thought Chappie and the lawyer would hear him and look out the window. Instead, they kissed.

It was a long kiss. Chappie's head went back and the lawyer's came forward. Her hands went to his hair and his went to somewhere I couldn't see. My palms became clammy with sweat. Before the kiss was over, Joey slipped and the lead from my hand and made a dash for the house. The window was a good three feet from the ground, and on a flying leap he went right through it. I'd never seen him jump like that, not even when he was a puppy. I'd have sworn he couldn't. But he sailed through that window as if sickness and age had never touched him.

I ran for the house, found the door unlocked, and flung it open.

The lawyer was on the floor trying to protect his face and throat with his arms, but Joey, licking furiously, worked around them. Chappie clutched Joey's collar with both hands, trying to pull him away. She may as well have tried to pull open a locked safe.

Because Joey was going mostly for the throat, I thought the lawyer had laryngitis. But his voice wasn't hoarse when he said,

"All *right,* dog, you've made your point. I won't kiss Chappie again until she says she'll marry me. Now let me up."

As if all Joey had wanted was that promise, he allowed Chappie to pull him away. She bent over Joey and slipped her arms around his neck, and I could see she was laughing.

The lawyer stood. He wiped the back of his hand across his throat. Looking at Joey, who was panting hard, he said, "That's quite a tongue. No shortage of saliva there, either."

Joey slipped to the floor, still panting. The lawyer looked at me. "Hi, you must be Gary. I'm Stephen Phillips."

He stuck his hand out but I didn't take it. I'd been distracted but wasn't now. "Chappie! Joey had a seizure cluster and my uncle wants to have him put down in the morning! And Karen's boyfriend knows he can cure illness and wants to steal him to get rich. We've got to get him out of Keystone right away!"

"He cures illness?" Stephen Phillips asked wonderingly. "This dog cures illness?"

"We have to take him away *now,* Chappie! We can't wait!"

Car headlights filled the room with chilling light and then died. An engine that I hadn't heard running was turned off and we were caught in a startling silence that Stephen Phillips broke by saying, "Someone's here."

Chappie reached for her notepad.

"No!" I hissed.

Her hand stalled on the pad, but her expression said, "Don't you *ever* tell me when to write a note."

"Let me handle it," said the lawyer. "If it's the uncle I'll reason with him, and if it's the boyfriend I'll put the fear of God in him."

They didn't understand. Feeling as if I would explode with frustration, I said, "You *can't* reason with my uncle!"

From outside came a thin voice wailing, "I'm sick. Oh, God, help me. I'm dying."

Joey ran out the door. We followed.

Karen, on her bare knees on the gravel drive, seemed to be gagging. Joey was licking her.

"Come on, Karen," called Doug from where he stood behind his open car door. "Bring him here."

I grabbed Joey's collar.

Karen moaned, "He made me drink poison so Joey would come to me."

"Karen? You hear me? I want that dog!"

"You're not going to get him!" I shouted. Then I saw the gun Doug was pointing over the car door.

Stephen Phillips stepped in front of me and called, "You can't have the dog because he isn't yours. I'm a lawyer. You've already got trouble. Don't compound it by—"

Doug shot him. He fell into me, making me lose my grip on Joey's collar. I regained my balance and saw Stephen on the ground in sort of a sitting position, with Chappie holding him and Joey licking him. Karen, whimpering, was crawling toward the cabin. I was the only one watching Doug come toward us, still pointing the gun. Was he going to kill us all?

Doug stopped behind Joey. His lips twitched nervously, and his eyes on mine held fear and anger. "Damn you. You should've let Karen bring him to me. I wasn't planning to shoot anyone. The gun went off accidentally. I swear it."

He leaned forward to reach for Joey's collar. Joey turned his head, then his body. I knew he was going to seizure. This was how he always moved when a seizure was coming on.

And he always collapsed before his mouth opened. But this time he didn't. This time his mouth opened while he was still standing. His mouth opened as wide as possible and then he lurched toward Doug and his jaws clamped shut around Doug's arm, above the hand that until this moment had been holding the gun.

Then Joey collapsed, pulling Doug, who was screaming in pain, down with him.

Wordlessly, I took off and ran the half mile to my relatives' house—heavily at first, reliving the horror of Doug coming at us with his gun. I'd stared at him in the disbelieving and hopeless way I imagine I would stare at the Angel of Death if he were a visible entity and clearly coming for me and those I loved.

But then the vision in my mind changed to Joey at the apogee of his leap through Chappie's window, and I flew. That vision carried me to my destination. It really did feel very much like flying.

I let myself in through the basement door that I'd left unlocked, and found Grandma Louise in the playhouse. I fell on my knees in front of her and grabbed one of her hands. "Grandma Louise, you have to save Chappie's boyfriend. Doug shot him. Give him your wish! Hurry!"

"What's his name?" she asked.

I stared dumbly at her, unable to remember.

"It won't work without his name, Gary," she said solemnly.

"It will! It has to!" I rose on my knees and clutched at her arms. "Just say, 'God, I want Chappie's boyfriend to live forever.' *Say it!*"

Quietly, with great sincerity in her voice, she said, "God, I want Chappie's boyfriend to live forever."

I had mumbled the words with her and let go of her arms afterwards.

"What's happened?" demanded my uncle from behind me. Not wanting to see him, I kept my eyes firmly on Grandma Louise, who was looking up at him. "Someone's been shot at Chappie's cabin, Ray. Call 911."

"Jesus." He ran out.

I was surprised when my aunt put her hands on my shoulders and asked, "Where's Joey?" I hadn't known she'd come down. The gentle way she asked the question told me she expected a sad answer.

"At Chappie's." My voice came out quavery. "He was having a seizure when I left. Karen's there too. She's sick."

"I'll get my keys," she said.

I started to get up. Aunt Ellen said very firmly, "Wait for me, Gary. Don't leave."

She'd never spoken to me that way before. I lowered my head to Grandma Louise's lap. She stroked my hair. My eyes rested on the Raggedy Ann doll that smiled day and night, year after year, through the dust-coated plastic bag where it lived with Karen's other dolls. I was almost crying. The thing was that I didn't really want to run back to the cabin, and was grateful to have been forbidden to leave. I thought that Grandma Louise's wish had worked and Chappie's boyfriend would live, but perhaps not Joey. Maybe he was having another seizure cluster right now and his body couldn't take it. Maybe when I got to the cabin he'd be dead. Dr. Meiners had told me long ago that even a single seizure, if severe enough, could cause death.

Uncle Ray and Aunt Ellen returned. She brought my rubber thongs. Uncle Ray said that someone had already called for an ambulance and the sheriff. Hearing this, I wondered if Joey had let go of Doug's arm before the sheriff got there. If he hadn't, he may have been . . .

I could not imagine it. I could not think of a bullet ripping through my Joey.

Uncle Ray drove. Aunt Ellen sat in back with me. No one talked.

A gray-haired man started walking toward us as we pulled up behind Doug's car. Joey didn't come to the car. I knew that if he was all right, he'd have come.

The man spoke through my uncle's window. "Are you folks the girl's parents?"

"Yes," my uncle said tightly.

"Well, she's okay. She's at the place I'm renting, just around the bend up there." He tilted his head over his shoulder. "My wife took her there and a deputy is with them, getting your daughter's story. The man who was shot and the kid who did the shooting and was bitten by the dog are at the hospital in Rapid City by now. The young woman who rents this cabin went with them."

Irrationally, I wondered if Chappie might have taken Joey along. That would explain his not being here to greet me.

"But our daughter's all right?" asked Aunt Ellen nervously.

He nodded. "Just shaken up, and a little sick to her stomach. Seems the boy made a cocktail of different kinds of liquor, seasoned it with salt and cooking oil, and made her drink it. But she'll be fine. The one who got shot'll be okay too, I'm pretty sure. He was talking incoherently, but talking. Said the doctors where he comes from told him he had cancer, so he tried not to fall in love."

"What about the dog?" asked Uncle Ray, and my knees started shaking. I put my hands on them but couldn't keep them still.

The man bent lower to the window and peered in sideways at me. "Was he your dog, son?"

Uncle Ray said, "This is Gary, our nephew. Joey . . . Joey was his dog."

"Well, Gary, the woman wouldn't let us leave Joey out here. She wanted him taken inside. So we did, and she covered him up. That's all I can tell you, except that I saw him and he looked peaceful."

Aunt Ellen touched my hand. I flinched. "Gary," she whispered. Then she and Uncle Ray got out of the car, leaving the doors open. I stayed. For as long as I remained in the car, I didn't have to believe Joey was dead. But the problem of my knees shaking would not go away. Stephen Phillips. That was Chappie's boyfriend's name. I'd been stupid to forget.

Aunt Ellen leaned down and said, "Gary, Mr. Snyder is going to take me to his cabin, to be with Karen. Uncle Ray will stay here."

I didn't answer, or look at her. She lingered a moment, then stepped back. Her shoes scrunched on the gravel as she started away with the man.

Uncle Ray opened my door.

"I'm not going in there," I said.

"I understand. Do you want to go home?"

Home! I got out of the car. "I'll walk," I said, looking away. "You can go to Karen."

"Gary, I want to be with you."

I turned on him. "You should be with Karen! She's your kid! I'm not! I'm not Alan! And my father never meant to hurt my mother! He'd have died before hurting her! It was an accident! It wasn't murder!"

I never saw a face crumple like Uncle Ray's did while I shouted these things at him. "Oh, God, you did hear," he said when I'd finished. "I know it was an accident. I know he didn't murder her. And I love your father. You've got to know that I love and respect him. I often hold him up . . . Aunt Ellen will tell you, Grandma Louise will . . . I hold your father up as a model for myself."

He made me sick. He'd have killed Joey if he could. How dare he say he modeled himself after my father. The words dog killer formed in my throat, but I left them there.

"Lawrence Frank is a successful father," said Uncle Ray. "I'm not. I envy him, but mostly I love him."

He made hating him too hard. I looked down.

"Gary, I'm going in to see Joey. Will you wait for me? Please say yes."

I said nothing.

"Try to wait," he said. "I'll need you to be here when I come out."

I looked up and said in tones angrier than I felt, "I'll go in. Alone. Don't come in."

The light had been left on in the cabin. Joey was on the hearth, where he had liked to be because the stones felt cool. Chappie had covered him with a quilt made by Mrs. Mooney. The quilt was folded over double. It covered him completely and was so thick I could barely make out his form. I decided that it wasn't necessary to see him. I could leave without seeing him dead.

Yes, I would do that.

I picked up the small bottle that Chappie had bought at an antique store and kept on her coffee table, turned it around in my hands and then shattered it against the wall. I swept a stack of paperbacks off the table, snatched one up and tore out a fistful of pages. I tried to rip open a throw pillow from the sofa, couldn't, and threw it down and mashed it with my foot.

I stomped over to the hearth and yanked the quilt away. Oh, my Joey was so beautiful. I knelt and buried my face in his fur.

And I cried.

CHAPTER 16

In The Analytical Realm
Of Adulthood

The night after Joey died my aunt and uncle lost their home in the flash flood that swept through the Black Hills, killing two-hundred and thirty-eight people.

We—Uncle Ray and I—had buried Joey in the woods near Chappie's cabin. We checked on the grave after the flood and found it undisturbed.

I flew home to Long Beach, to stay with the Mooneys until my father's year in Japan was up. Chappie followed, with Stephen, when he was recovered enough from his wound to travel. After they married, they returned to Keystone. The town has been their home ever since.

The reason why Stephen had refused to go on a date with Chappie when she asked was that he had just that week been diagnosed with cancer of the thyroid. He didn't want to begin a relationship when he was sick and might die. But having already fallen in love with Chappie, he finally traveled to South Dakota to tell her so.

When new x-rays were taken of Stephen's thyroid after the shooting, and no cancer was found, everyone else thought he'd been the victim of a misdiagnosis. But I had seen Stephen on the floor being licked by Joey, and I knew otherwise.

I received a letter at the Mooneys' from Daphne. She wrote that she'd heard about Joey and was sorry for my loss. I answered the letter and we became pen pals. One of the first things she told me in our decade-long correspondence was that she hated her name. "One boy in school calls me Daffy Duck and it drives me wild. I want to kill him when he does that. But my mom says when I'm sixteen I can choose a new name for myself if I still want, and we'll have it changed legally. I know I'll want to and I've picked the name. It's Dee. Do you like it? I'm swearing you to secrecy, Gary. You're the only friend I've told."

To Daphne, I confided the whole story of Joey's magic powers. She wrote back that she believed every word.

And what do I believe, now that I'm a sometimes-weary veterinarian? I believe in reason, which tells me that the blood on my hand the night of my sixth birthday probably came from a superficial wound in Joey's mouth, and that earaches felt by children on chilly mornings do not always materialize into illness.

Reason also tells me that a child peering at a dove under a shrub might see a healthy outstretched wing as a broken one.

And so on and so on. Unleash reason and there's no stopping it.

Chappie swears that the bruise she had on her knee the day we met was an old one that she'd already forgotten about. She claims that she didn't swear this when I was a child because she'd wanted to spare me the pain of disbelief. (The note she wrote that day when we walked in the park and Joey licked one old man's fingers and another's foot was a ruse; she hadn't believed that Joey would suffer if I told people he had healing powers, but that I would.)

Every question I've asked myself about Joey since joining Chappie in the analytical realm of adulthood has at least two answers, and one requires my stalwart childhood faith to leap across my squirming adult intellect.

The other answer is the one that would always be chosen by those who would love to answer for the Minot Chamber of Commerce its piquant question: Why not Minot? It's the answer that makes sense.

For example, was Joey's refusal to go near my mother in the hospital because curing her was beyond his limits? No. He was afraid. Afraid of her hurt. Of the odors of her dying. Of the hospital's forbidding strangeness.

And did Grandma Louise's eyes really get better because Joey licked them? Again, no. She only believed they were better because I put the idea in her head. (Even a little faith would work wonders for a person who's already enjoyed a long life believing she poured tea for God.)

All the getting wells and getting betters, the vanished bites and bruises, can be chalked up to other sources of healing, or they may not have happened at all.

Or, and I told myself this as I flew to South Dakota to see Chappie's new puppy, you could give the nod to Joey.

I do. I saw him lick my father's forehead after the accident, and I saw how quickly the laceration healed. I was at an age to know about gashes. It was a mean cut and it shouldn't have mended that fast. I saw Joey fly through the window of Chappie's cabin to lick a stranger who, through x-ray, had been diagnosed with cancer. Minutes before Joey made that heroic leap, he'd had trouble standing and walking. He'd just suffered neurological devastation. His life was about to end. Why did Joey do it if not to work his magic once more and save Stephen's life?

Stephen met me at the airport. "Chappie stayed home with the kids," he said. "They've organized a competition in honor of Uncle Gary's visit."

I smiled. Chappie with four children, and past fifty. In my mind she was always somewhere between twenty and thirty, wearing white shorts.

"How are Dee and the kids?" Stephen asked as we walked to his car. "They're great," I answered and asked how Grandma Louise was. She'd been living with Chappie and Stephen since my Aunt Ellen and Uncle Ray moved to Florida.

"For a nonagenarian, Louise is amazing," said Stephen. "She could outlive us all."

Which wouldn't surprise me, I thought with some glee.

Grandma Louise, in her wheelchair, was outside the house in Keystone when we drove up the driveway. With her were my first love, her four children, four dogs, and a sky full of stars.

Each dog was freshly groomed and beribboned, and standing in front of the Phillips child who was its designated owner-handler. I avoided looking at the German shepherd pup, although I knew it was silly of me.

"Uncle Gary, this is our first annual dog show," said one of the children, "You pick the best of show."

Chappie held the blue ribbon I was to award. I hugged her, then bent to kiss Grandma Louise. She slowly reached a hand up and caressed my hair, reminding me of the night when Joey died and Stephen Phillips lived.

I whispered in her ear, "You really saved the wish for yourself, didn't you?"—and had a moment of worry that the glib question might have offended.

"You won't find out from me," she whispered back. "But I will tell you that my money's on the spaniel."

A bad bet. Ceremoniously, I handed the blue ribbon to Chappie's beaming six-year-old, whose real name is Christopher. A kid nicknamed Rumpkin has enough problems without my being biased against his puppy because of the tears in my eyes.

Stephen, in gentle tones, said, "Remind you of an old friend?"

I nodded.

"We got him at the animal shelter. A foreign fellow dropped him off there the night before we went to look for a puppy. He had to go back to his own country and couldn't take a dog with him."

About The Author

Cindy Victor is the author of six contemporary romance novels, a romance novel of nineteenth-century Korea, a suspense novel, three greyhound novels, and two breed books (*The Essential Guide for the Greyhound Lover,* and *German Shepherd Dog: Lifelong Care for Your Dog).* Her short stories have appeared in *Confrontation, Greensboro Review, William and Mary Review, Kansas Quarterly, Karamu, South Dakota Review,* and *Phoebe, a Journal of Literary Arts.*

Born in Minneapolis, Minnesota, she has lived in California, Hawaii, South Dakota, and on Guam. She now lives in Woodbury, Minnesota with her husband, Gary, and their retired racing greyhound, Bruce.

30113153R00110

Made in the USA
Charleston, SC
02 June 2014